CHILDREN'S SPACES

CHILDREN'S SPACES

50 Architects & Designers Create Environments for the Young

Molly & Norman McGrath

Foreword
by Ivan Chermayeff

WILLIAM MORROW AND COMPANY, INC.   NEW YORK

Acknowledgments

WE WOULD LIKE TO THANK the contributors to this book—the designers both professional and amateur, the architects—and our friends who shared our enthusiasm for this project. In particular we wish to thank Susan Grant Lewin of *House Beautiful* and Rod Freebairn-Smith for their invaluable leads. To Pam Hatch whose foresight started the book on its way to publication, our gratitude, as well as to our patient and supportive editor, Narcisse Chamberlain.

The quality of the black-and-white photographs in this book is due in no small measure to the talent of Mike Shiffrin who did all the black and white printing and processing.

Frontispiece: The Box, by Henry Smith-Miller and Michael Rubin; see pages 180-183, 188.

Book Design by Lucy M. Fehr

Library of Congress Cataloging in Publication Data

Main entry under title:

Children's spaces.

    1. Children's rooms. 2. Interior decoration.
I. McGrath, Molly. II. McGrath, Norman.
NK2117.C4C47   747'.77   78-15324
ISBN 0-688-03329-6

Printed in the United States of America.
First Edition
1 2 3 4 5 6 7 8 9 10

Foreword

The not-so-extraordinary thing about children is that they are people. Younger, shorter, and less experienced, but with the advantage of not having acquired a great surfeit of useless knowledge which might render them incapable of intelligently ordering their surroundings.

Children, by and large, react naturally to their own inner urges, directly and without inhibitions. They crawl, climb, jump, build, destroy, play and study on the floor, taking up new activities quickly and abandoning them even faster. They laugh freely, cry at slight discomforts and small hurts, whine if thwarted, complain of anything which is not immediately made available to them, and let the older and taller guardians of their existence know of their impatience.

Children fall asleep quickly. The seemingly boundless energy just runs out. (Thank God!) And they drift, in seconds, into coma—upside down, their heads hanging in uncomfortable-appearing postures. Then they awaken to make known their demands and to experiment with noises indicating that they have even further demands to make.

The best spaces designed for children account for the way children are, generally and specifically.

Architects, interior designers, furniture designers, artists and decorators who try to do something positive for their own children's spaces or their clients' children's spaces are successful when they concentrate on the occupants, not the owners, remembering too that children grow and change quickly.

A child's space is special and familiar territory in which to hide and seek things. All children, of any age, need places to display to themselves and their world their priceless and valueless treasures, mementoes and souvenirs. A child's private space can be viewed as an opportunity to encourage imaginative change.

Children need somewhere to stick and pin things up. Mostly they need to post their discoveries, their loves and their aspirations, and to be able to put them away when there are too many or when they change their minds.

There must be places for heroes and heroines.
Space to foul; room to move; soft corners to fall asleep in.
Storage, lots of it, for incredible accumulations.
Color and light.
Not a classroom.
No images that won't erase.
No one wants to live in somebody else's personal expression.
No invasions of privacy.
A *tabula rasa*, because children don't have to be reinvented.

Ivan Chermayeff
New York
1978

This book is for our children, Helen and Colin, and for their grandfather, Munroe Wade. It is also dedicated to Raymond McGrath, who encouraged us to do the book, but did not live to see it become a reality.

Contents

The classic interior designer can
maintain the significant architectural
constants of a design concept—space,
light, simplicity and variety—while
providing satisfaction for a client's
desires and dreams.

—C. Ray Smith
New York Times Magazine, 6/20/76

Introduction

Children's rooms have changed more in the last twenty years than any other room in the house. Not so long ago, a child's room was considered perfectly adequate if it was well ventilated and lit, furnished with a bed, a table or desk and chair, and sufficient storage space for clothes and toys. Then came the notion of a small world designed specifically for a child, quite separate from the rest of the house. The idea may have sprung from the same design thinking that in the 1960s inspired grown-ups to build for themselves womblike places to be alone. Or it may be that busy modern parents, rather like some Victorians who relegated their children to the nursery, want to create a place so ideally suited to their child's every need and wish that he will be content to spend long periods of time there.

More than one hundred years ago, the Industrial Revolution introduced machines to do the jobs that had required so many hands before. Scores of working-class people became available to help wealthier families keep their households running smoothly, thus allowing many wives and mothers to get out of the house. It was, in most respects, a harmonious arrangement for everyone concerned. But two World Wars and subsequent economic history changed all that. In the decades after 1914, servants became more and more the exception rather than the rule, middle-class women went back to their kitchens, and nurseries became simply children's rooms—places to sleep and do homework or to endure childhood illnesses. Children spent more of their time in other parts of the house, in rooms where Mother could keep an eye on them.

Now the women's movement has liberated many housewives once again, not to visit museums and dressmakers or to do volunteer work, but to pursue careers and salaries sometimes equal to their husbands'. There are signs of this additional income in the children's room, perhaps to ease Mother's conscience for not being there herself.

Whether Mother is in charge of the nursery, or Nanny, or the baby-sitter, the environment parents provide for their child tells the child a great deal about what is important to the grown-ups in his life and what they want to share with him. The objects and atmosphere that surround the young child give him a good idea of what is expected of him; in subtle ways he learns how to act toward the objects and the people in a way that pleases those who care for him. While the child's environment in the home may be designed to please the child, it is, as well, a tangible expression of the parents' hopes and dreams for that child.

Whatever the reasoning behind the idea of environments for children, their first appearance coincided with new design concepts for materials for teaching children and new kinds of games and toys to entertain them. In the late 1950s, psychologists made us especially aware of the importance of intellectual stimulation in the first three years of life. Parents became eager to buy every possible game, toy, body-building structure to create the perfect early-learning environment. During the Lyndon Johnson Administration in the 1960s, public schools received huge infusions of federal money to purchase educational materials. School-age children came home with descriptions of elaborate audiovisual equipment and mechanical teaching devices. It did not take long for parents of this technologically sophisticated generation to accept the idea of a TV set in the children's room along with the child-size record player. Now it is not unusual for older children to have their own stereos and tape decks, even videotape machines, to enjoy in the privacy of their own soundproof space, out of adult earshot.

Yet, children who live in tailor-made environments do not always want to isolate themselves from the rest of the family. It is lonely to be confined to one small world, even if it is custom-designed for you. So, particularly in families where there are several children, the "environments" may intersect, often in quite unpredictable ways.

Some of the environments we show in this book were designed to clients' detailed specifications. Others, particularly those in architects' own homes, just evolved. These often reflect better than the "designed" ones current developments in thinking about space for children. The subject of environments for children happens, we have also found, to coincide with a period of renewed interest on the part of architects in interior design. Architects formerly concerned primarily with the external forms of structures are becoming more involved in interiors, thereby reestablishing a unity that is appropriate in the design professions. It is not surprising that some of these people should be experimenting in their own homes, particularly in the children's rooms, where challenges to ingenuity and imagination are endless.

We hope it will be useful to other parents to see what is possible in children's rooms and, with the help of good photographs, to find new ways to bring fantasy and fun as well as practical solutions to everyday problems into the spaces where children live.

—MOLLY AND NORMAN McGRATH

CHILDREN'S SPACES

A CHILD'S WORLD

The environment of the very young child is its home—the space, the people, and the objects in it. Within this small and quite private world, the first steps in life are taken.

Since the turn of the century, when Sigmund Freud advanced his theories concerning early childhood and development, psychologists have debated the relative importance of heredity and environment. The controversy is hardly resolved. As the Canadian psychologist Donald Hebb put it, "Deciding this matter is like trying to determine how much of the area of a field is due to its length and how much to its width." Almost the only conclusion that can be drawn is that the two are so closely linked that it is impossible to determine the precise effect of each in forming the final result.

But parents know more now than they did fifty years ago about ways to make a child's first environment a warm, welcoming place. Designers, psychologists, and toy manufacturers have all worked to discover what most effectively stimulates and amuses a new baby. They have ascertained that an infant responds in perceptible ways to bright colors (some more than others), to movement of an object such as a mobile over the crib, to noises both pleasant and unpleasant, to different shapes and textures, and, when the child is older, to variously shaped spaces. Inspired by these findings, parents often bring fantasy and humor as well as common sense to the design of their child's first environment. Sometimes they deliberately plan it to be temporary, knowing that when the child is older, there will be another kind of room, designed differently, to suit the child's different needs.

Not all families can undertake to change their child's room frequently, but a true nursery, resembling a page out of a child's storybook, is the first step for those who feel strongly that a child's world is a special kind of space.

Noel Jeffrey

To create a successful child's room means, to me, to create a total environment. In doing this, I try to work with the available space to create an area in which the child can grow, learn, play, and develop his or her own potential. The spaces used have to be interesting and related to the actual way children live and play.

One element that pleases all children is color—they respond to it in many ways. I try to incorporate a lot of color in the rooms I design. As part of the use of color, I find supergraphics effective—large images drawn from learning experiences or fantasy painted on the walls. These supergraphics can be made up of alphabet letters, numbers, squares, rectangles, or circles. Clouds, rainbows, butterflies, and small animals can be depicted, too. These elements help stir the lively imaginations of children.

Color can also be a prominent feature of furniture design. I like to use built-in furniture which shapes the space—furniture made of natural wood with bright color accents. As the child grows older, the wood tones remain appropriate, and the colors can be changed to give a more grown-up appearance. The built-in furniture should be flexible and scaled for children. For example, a desk can be built low and then elevated as the child grows. But from the start all storage spaces for books and toys should be easily accessible and easily managed by the child. Blackboards and bulletin boards can be important parts of the built-in design; they give the child a chance to make his own contributions to the appearance of his room.

Another way of using space effectively is to give children different levels to play on, encouraging a feeling that the room has more space, and has different areas for sleep, play, and study. If needed, the undersides of the levels can be used for additional, unobtrusive storage. But whether or not the floor space has several levels, I think that all floor surfaces should be smooth, uncarpeted, and easily cleanable.

Sometimes it is desirable to have a small carpet around the bed to define that area within the larger space. This area should definitely have bright lights for reading, and, in fact, all the areas in a child's room should have good illumination. An architect's lamp can provide controllable lighting that is highly suitable for a child's work space.

Finally, there should be some provision made, if space allows, for a child's room to be shared with a friend. When possible, an extra bed is a welcome addition. The juxtaposition of the beds, for jumping from one to the other, or as a design feature, can provide another element of interest. Of course, with enough space, there is also a chance to include ever-popular gym equipment—rings, bars, and trapezes that can provide diversion on a rainy day. Combined carefully, these design ideas can help a child feel that his room is a major part of his world.

The Interlubke system along one wall of Joanna's room provides a variety of storage spaces for toys and clothes. The slide-out wire baskets at one end and the stacking storage cylinders from Beylerian, Ltd., in New York offer easy access to items Joanna uses often. The shelves and drop-leaf panel on the left rotate to reveal a full-size bed that folds down from the reverse side for occasional overnight guests.

Tennis buffs can encourage their children to
have Lilliputian dreams in giant-sneaker beds
designed by Michelle Gamm Clifton. The tops
lace up snugly on cold winter nights and
everything is washable!

I guess we were just plain bored with what was being offered in the way of children's equipment and furniture. Since children's rooms are usually small, with beds taking up much of the limited space, we wanted to put together a unit that could function as a climbing structure, clubhouse, hideout, boat, or spaceship as well as a bed.

—PENNY HULL

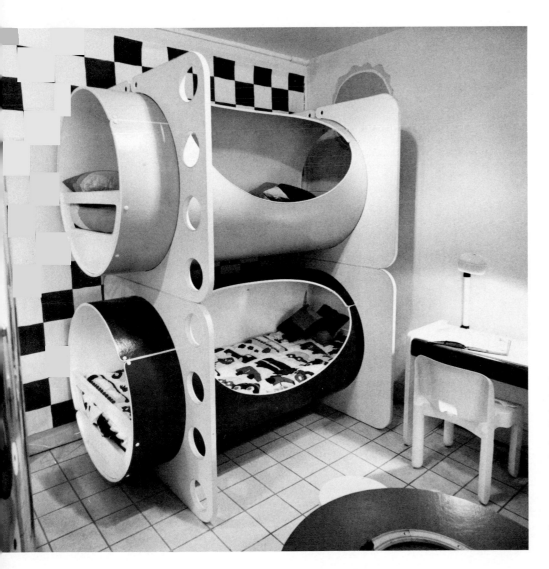

Vinyl-covered Sono tubes (spirally laminated fiber forms) are the basis for this bunk-bed system devised by architect Jim Hull and his wife, Penny, who also designs the coordinated fabrics. The vertical panels with climbing holes are made of plastic-coated, high-density particle board. The bunk system is one example of Toobline furniture, available in the H.U.D.D.L.E. stores in California. The Hull children's drawings were the inspiration for the fabric design ''Traffic,'' shown on the lower bed.

Iris Vanderputten and Karen Sevell-Greenbaum, who call their partnership Whimsical Walls, have a magic touch with nurseries. Guided by the clients' suggestions, the two women can transform an ordinary room into a fairy-tale garden with giant toadstools in rainbow colors or anywhere in dreamland that a child might like to go. Working from scale drawings, Iris and Karen use latex paint on clean, preferably white, walls. The murals are "layered" to include forms and subtle shades that the child will notice as he or she grows older.

Owen Beenhouwer

I don't think any of the children's rooms I have designed started out to be an "environment." They became environments for a variety of reasons: a need for flexibility or multiple use, a desire for a special bunk or playhouse arrangement, an aversion to manufactured children's furniture. All the functions are brought together by a common scale, suited to the occupant of the room, and by color tying together and interlocking the various elements and shapes.

I was asked to provide a bunk bed and ample storage space in the small room I designed for David (see page 186). As the design progressed, I could see that I was making an elaborate climbing frame, with ladder rungs to reach the bed placed at a princely height above the storage shelves and clothes closet. We put in a rope ladder up to the bunk platform, with a fireman's pole (just out of the photo to the left) for a quick return to ground level.

The larger room for the two girls, Angie and Kaja, already had a portable slide. We added a very open and light bunk that is fun to climb on, plus a two-story house with ladders, a door, a light, and a window that serves as a store counter or puppet theater—all airy and painted white to unify the many colors in the doll clothes and blankets (see page 22).

In Andrew's large dark room I tried to lighten the entire space with bright colors: white enlivened by yellow and orange (see page 147). To achieve a greater sense of space, I placed all elements around the edge of the room and kept them light and open in appearance—open shelving and storage units, climbing platforms with holes cut out. Two ladders lead above the closets to the bunk, which extends into the only dark corner that is actually rather like a tree house, a secret place. From there a child can go down the slide to the bed below.

Sarah's room required the most compression of elements to leave some open play space (see pages 26-27). The bed drawer pulls out into the only corner of the room free for play during the day. When it is not being slept in, the bed can be pushed away. (It rolls under the couch inside the playhouse.) The upper platform, at the top of the ladder, is big enough for a standard mattress to accommodate a visiting friend. Sarah can hide inside the house, play with her dolls, or climb on the framework—it's sturdy enough. The desk stands partly free, for use as a table, and is adjustable so as to be the right height for Sarah as she grows.

A child is eager to learn and wants to explore his world by using it, by choosing what he wants to do, by touching and manipulating. When the room/environment invites this kind of imaginative participation and suggests but does not limit play, it is successful.

These structures in Angie and Kaja
Beenhouwer's room offer opportunities for
exercise as well as for quiet play and
sleeping. Both units stand free of the walls,
and, like many of Owen Beenhouwer's other
structures for children, they can be taken
apart and reassembled elsewhere.
Deliberately dominant, surface-mounted
electrical conduits with industrial light sockets
provide added design detail.

23

Michelle Gamm Clifton

Before I made Alexander's farm, I had done a jungle room for a family with eight children and a few rooms with circus themes and garden motifs. As a sculptor who likes to work in soft materials, I've always wanted to re-create a farm. I never actually asked my son, Alexander, if he wanted a farm, but he had never said he *wouldn't* like one. That was all the encouragement I needed. (See page 28.)

I started Alexander's room when he was two years old. I chose Tri-wall as the material for the basic construction of the farm. Tri-wall is three laminations of corrugated cardboard. It is durable and very inexpensive and it comes in many sizes. The sheets I bought were 48 by 54 inches. I used it for the structural part of the bed and for the outside walls of the barn. The dresser is old, so I decided to paint it right into my design. The slide is Masonite, painted with washable latex paint to match the barn. I used leftover carpeting to denote different areas of the farmyard. I wanted to use green indoor-outdoor carpeting, but as we had other remnants, I worked with those. We bought a few feet of fence and added the rope swing so Alexander could exercise indoors even on rainy days. The total cost of doing the whole room was only about $200.

I think children's rooms should be as much fun, as full of humor, imagination, and fantasy as possible. When I do a room for someone else's child, I usually have some idea of what the parents want. The next step is to talk with the child. By the time I do that, I often have an idea vaguely formulated in my mind to discuss with the parents. I am always very interested in what the child wants, and I believe the child's ideas should be worked into the design scheme as much as possible.

You might say that I see children's rooms as an excuse for the parents to get together with their children to do something they've always wanted to do, but somehow don't have the courage to do in their living room. I would love to do whole rooms for adults in a fanciful way. I have done a Manhattan environment of this type, with a couch that is part of a small-scale model of the New York skyline. It stands now in the Museum of the City of New York. Unfortunately though, while it has become socially acceptable to have some crazy things in your living room, most people are not ready to commit themselves to a totally built-in, sculptured environment. So I will continue to indulge my imagination by doing rooms for children and people who are young at heart.

Four-year-old Joanna's rainbow-wrapped bed is bordered by silhouettes of bushes cut out of green-painted cork on plywood panels. Another piece of cork-plywood near the bed serves as a bulletin board. Colored balloons and butterflies and a box kite with Joanna's name on it festoon the walls and ceiling in this room by Noel Jeffrey. The quilt is made by Ann Oestreicher in Toronto.

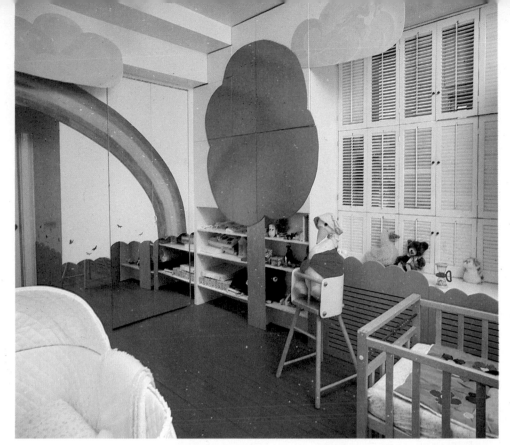

In Noel Jeffrey's nursery for his son, Gerard, a rainbow painted on one wall brings color and fantasy into the room. Plywood cutout clouds with animal faces float by near the ceiling. As Gerard crawls on the floor, he can see himself in Plexiglas mirrors cut in the shape of bushes. More bushes, cut out of plywood, conceal the radiator under the window. A bed for Gerard's nurse folds down from an Interlubke unit not shown in this photograph.

Sara's bed, mounted on wheels, rolls out below the open shelves on one side of this multipurpose unit by architect Owen Beenhouwer. When not in use, the bed, fully made up, parks in a space below a second bed inside the structure, completely hidden from view. The ladder leads to the highest level, with a third bed on it.

Using remnants of fabric, Tri-wall cardboard, and latex paint, Michelle Gamm Clifton has made a fantasy farmyard for her son. Alexander reaches his sleeping loft by ladder; he can slide down in the morning if he is late for breakfast. The vinyl cow makes a comfortable sofa with a seat of vinyl grass. The carpeting is the appropriate color to represent grass and dirt, the trash can is silver-painted vinyl, and the fence posts are real.

Architect Owen Beenhouwer designed this all-purpose unit for Sarah, the two-year-old daughter of a Manhattan couple. Big enough for Sarah to stand in, it can accommodate two overnight guests—one inside the playhouse and one on top. The bubblelike portholes are fun to look through and the plastic storage trays keep toys tidy yet easily accessible. Beenhouwer planned Sarah's house to "grow with her." The unit has, in fact, moved with Sarah and her family to a new apartment (see pages 26-27), where it works as well as it did in the original room.

Angled into one corner of Nila's room, this combination playhouse/sleeping/storage unit by Owen Beenhouwer is yellow and white with a bright-blue-carpeted stair and upper deck. The entrance is to the right, and the small curtained window doubles as a puppet stage. A blue Formica desk curves into the room a few feet away from the playhouse.

A ROOM TO GROW IN

Designers and design-minded parents, particularly those who live in urban areas, have created a great variety of interior environments for children. They fill them with the things they dreamed of having as children and things they think their children will enjoy. In most cases it is probably true that the rooms reflect the parents' values more than the children's; designers' children's rooms quite clearly show the parents' interest in forming the taste of their children by surrounding them with good colors, strong forms, and well-made toys and furniture.

We were interested to discover, after two years of gathering material for this book, what a gold mine of ideas and solutions New York City is to problems of designing domestic environments for children. We surmise that this is due not only to the great number of designers and architects in the area, but also to the need that parents feel in this super-urban center to compensate for their children's lack of freedom to run out-of-doors, to play in empty lots, to wander freely without supervision. Dense population in a city where there is a high premium on space seems to call for resourcefulness, as much as the frontier did.

Quite possibly, some designed environments for children are desperate attempts to persuade the child to stay at home, not to hurry too quickly into the dangerous world beyond his doorstep. Built-in environments may be a way of saying, "Stay here for a while in this world we have made for you. It's more pleasant here, and safer, than it is out there."

On the other hand, we have also noticed a trend, perhaps more among architects than designers, to involve the child in the shaping of his own environment. These people have made an effort, particularly with their own children, not only to consult the child with regard to priorities and preferences, but actually to engage the child in handling the materials that will form his small world. In this way the child gains a feeling of participation in what is being done for him and a sense of sharing in the responsibility for it.

Thus, rooms for children can be planned to promote character development as well as to meet the playing, climbing, imaginative needs of the child at several different stages of growth. The design problems of making such a space to grow in are many and complex—and so are the solutions.

. . . Children, remember, start out life smaller than adults, in a far smaller world, limited at first to their cribs, then expanding as their mobility increases. Experiences of space and light and motion and the opportunity for things to happen are all new in their lives. Teachers of children in slum areas note that environmental deprivation, the absence of experiences with the world around them, is as crippling a limitation as the lack of food and formal education. That this sensual deprivation is not limited to childhood or poverty can be attested to by adults who frequent Holiday Inns. But the rewards for giving children the chance to open up their senses should be evident.

It is worth adding, too, that many children grow big before they grow well coordinated, and asking them to mince around in small spaces hemmed in by delicate objects may just be unreasonable. It is also true that childhood is a period of rapid change, and it doesn't do to plan too precisely for the requirements of a nine-year-old in a house he may not move into until he is ten.

From The Place of Houses *by Charles Moore, Donlyn Lyndon, Gerald Allen. Copyright ©1974 by Charles Moore, Donlyn Lyndon, Gerald Allen. Reprinted by permission of Holt, Rinehart & Winston, Publishers.*

This room planned by Charles Moore with Richard Oliver for a young boy combines the cozy atmosphere of a traditional room with the more contemporary idea of a raised bed with built-in storage space. The sheets on Grant's bed pick up the jungle motif of the wallpaper design called "Toile de Juillet."

John Saladino

A child's room should present the possibility of many environments. Before this can happen, the designer must overcome the tyranny of a six-plane space. The floor and four walls are archenemies that have to be confronted in order to release the imagination. But they can be made to work for the designer and to trigger the child's imagination and stimulate all kinds of fantasy. A catwalk along one end of a boy's room could tempt him to be a pirate on a Spanish galleon. Or he could be Batman, Superman—whoever he pleases.

The floor is probably the most difficult part of the problem. Should it be practical, cushioned for a lower decibel level in this noisiest part of the house? Or should it be hard and smooth so a child can dribble a ball or spread out a model railroad on it? I've come to believe that the ideal situation for the flooring in a child's room is not wall-to-wall carpeting, but a combination of hard surface and area carpet. It is useful to have at least some uncarpeted floor in the part of the room where the child plays with messy things such as paint and clay. In some other part of the room, I recommend a round carpet that can be easily removed and laundered. A carpet like this can mark a special zone: a little girl's dining room or a boy's raft. Children will find a hundred uses for it.

Baroque painters often painted ceilings to make space transcend its physical limits. We can do this in children's rooms, too. A child in a city apartment should have a special ceiling in his room. When he's lying in bed at night he should be able to imagine that he is in the South Seas, or sailing through space. A ceiling doesn't have to be white and ordinary. Why not hang a collection of kites or flags from it? Have footprints going up the wall and across the ceiling. These things would help to counteract the tyranny of the fixed plane.

Beds should be part of the landscape of the room. They should be much more than places to sleep. They can be aviaries or captain's walks or building parapets for Superman. There's no reason why a bed has to take the shape of a bed. It could be a boat with a mattress, or a sports car with a mattress where the seats usually are. You don't have to buy miniature adult furniture for a child.

Children's rooms need more lighting than adult bedrooms, possibly as much as a kitchen. Children use their room as a workplace, so I think the light level should be at clerical efficiency level. Young eyes should not get damaged in the process of learning the alphabet.

There are a number of sources of supply for unusual items that work very well in children's rooms. Sweet's Catalog lists such engaging items as a multishelved rolling cart with baskets that are marvelous for storing toys. The cart is really intended for a swimmers' locker room; a swimmer can put his clothing in the basket, then push the basket back into the metal-frame superstructure and lock it. The thing is perfect for a child. Other good sources are hospital-supply houses. They make totally serviceable, damage-proof shelving, tables, carts with rubber bumpers and overscaled wheels.

A little girl's room I designed (see pages 34-35, 45) has some touches that are both whimsical and practical. There are steps with storage units inside. A ramp and raised floor bring up the level of the room, allowing a four-year-old to be "in scale" with a built-in table. Later, when she's eight or nine, the raised floor and ramp can be removed, thereby making the built-in table still in scale. This is one way of making a room flexible enough to work through many stages of the child's growth.

In this room by John Saladino there is a place for every favorite object of childhood. In a few years, with no structural changes, the room will work equally well for an older girl.

John Saladino's room for a little girl is perfect for making the transition from infancy to childhood. A stepped, painted panel on the left wall complements the shelving at the right. The gray Pirelli tile on the floor gives an architectural look to the space and is a good sound absorber.

This room designed by John Saladino does double duty for two preteen-aged boys. Industrial shelving provides readily accessible storage and display space for the boys' favorite objects, games, and books. Additional storage for clothes and other gear is provided in drawers, closets, and in the plastic storage tower with sliding doors on the far left. The walls are covered with painted cork so that displays can be changed frequently without damaging wall surfaces.

One way to deal with the problem of spills and stains in a child's room is to incorporate them into the design of the room. Carol Levy has done this in a room in which bands of red and blue explode on a yellow wall, spattering onto a floor that reminds one of a Jackson Pollock painting. The red and blue bands even continue across the window on the multicolored Levolor blinds. The floor is painted parquet with a polyurethane finish.

Myron Goldfinger

Children are so much more inventive and creative than we are. Rather than impose our wills and design ideas on them by doing huge supergraphics on the walls or following a certain theme throughout the room, I believe in giving children a structural framework which they can fill with their own favorite objects and displays. In this way the child participates in the design of his or her environment and the room clearly reflects that child's personality.

In the rooms I design for adults, I like to have some control over the final total effect. I don't feel that it is enough to structure or restructure a space, then make no further contribution to it as a designer. But I feel differently about what I do for children. Somehow their own treasures and talismans seem the most appropriate decoration for the rooms they live in. Given the right basic structure or framework, the accessories can change as the child grows older. The puppets and dolls will be replaced by footballs and stereo equipment, and the basic room will work in new ways.

Mexican quarry tile adds color and warmth to this all-white room by architect Myron Goldfinger, furnished by June Goldfinger. The balconylike space has an enclosed spiral stair and sloping ceiling. The oddly shaped door to the upper hallway follows the line of the hallway ceiling beyond—exactly opposite to the angle of the ceiling in the children's room.

Opposite:
Myron Goldfinger has provided a neat, one-piece bed unit, combining both toy and clothes storage and a desk, for eight-year-old Nina in this New Jersey house. White Formica is used throughout. The orange bedcover with white stripes and the girl's own toys and posters add colorful touches to her room.

Mark's room, designed by Noel Jeffrey, has three major zones: one large playroom (foreground) with an adjacent bedroom (to the left), and a bathroom (right). The central space is framed in a broad band of green that travels across the floor and ceiling and up the walls. Geometric forms painted in high-gloss shades of red, blue, and yellow mirror each other on the floor and ceiling. Panels of tinted Plexiglas filter the track lights, adding still more color.

Noel Jeffrey's client wanted a four-poster bed for her three-year-old daughter. Jeffrey designed a simple wooden four-poster that looks contemporary and can be made to look more frilly if, later on, the little girl wants a bed of more traditional style.

The circular opening cut out of wallboard frames a mural painted on the roller blinds. In this mural, as in the ones on the wall and ceiling, the sky is glossy blue and the clouds are painted matte white to make them stand out. Interlubke units on the wall opposite the bed provide closet and shelf space for clothes and toys.

Noel Jeffrey designed this room for two brothers. Each boy has his own bed and bookcase, separated by a low cork bulletin board partition. The room is further divided by the high storage unit at left, incorporating a wall-mounted blackboard, built-in lighting, and a band of blue-painted floor. The multicolored horizontal wall stripe, continuous on all four walls and across the Levolor blinds, visually draws the room together as a single unified space.

In this room by Noel Jeffrey for a six-year-old boy called A.J., there is a place for everything, even a visiting friend who might choose to spend the night. The acrylic carpet is grass green; the bed and study units are natural wood with a French-waxed finish. The mural is made of cork and serves as a bulletin board. The sturdy supports invite climbing.

At the far end of the room by the window, the work-study unit provides space to spread out books and papers and to store them, in drawers at either end of the desk, or in the openings just above it. There is more storage space above the openings on the other side of the desk. The center section of the desk is adjustable in height as A.J. grows older.

California brothers share this room where two rainbows meet. The mural was designed by Ruth and Brian McKinney. The combination beds-and-desk unit designed by Jim and Penny Hull for their Toobline series is made from natural southern pine and Sono tubing. The fabric pattern on the bedcover is called "Target." Designed by Penny Hull, the material and the Toobline furniture are available in the H.U.D.D.L.E. shops in California.

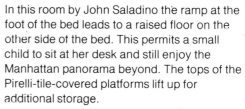

In this room by John Saladino the ramp at the foot of the bed leads to a raised floor on the other side of the bed. This permits a small child to sit at her desk and still enjoy the Manhattan panorama beyond. The tops of the Pirelli-tile-covered platforms lift up for additional storage.

A trio of staggered windows with bright-red Levolor blinds and a vertical alcove complete with ladder immediately distinguish this room designed by Charles Moore with Richard Oliver. The ladder provides access to a tower similar to the one seen through the window and also to vertical storage space on the opposite side of the alcove.

Color and form are the only decorative devices used in this room by Charles Gwathmey for young Robbie. The desk, bed, and rounded cabinet are actually three separate units, though together they look like one integral, sculptured piece. The wall is dark green and bare, not only because the color appeals to Robbie, but because he likes to throw a ball against it now and then. In an otherwise similar room, Robbie's brother, Eric, uses his blue wall as a tennis backboard (see page 62).

Alexandra Stoddard's room for her daughter reflects the little girl's delight in appealing textures, shapes, and colors. She and a friend can do their homework together in one corner of the room, or enjoy a game on the floor where there is lots of free space. Storage boxes under the spare bed make tidying easier.

The uncluttered surfaces in this environment by Sharon Lee Ryder lend themselves not only to work and play but to flights of fancy. Douglas can pretend he is in command of a medieval fortress, or castle, or galleon . . . or he can just enjoy being alone in his own private place where only the chosen few are allowed to go. Below the desk where the aquarium is located is a secret panel providing access to a space under the platforms that can be used for storage or as an additional hiding place for Douglas.

Robert Rhodes

I don't have a philosophy of design for children's rooms. During the conceptual stage of a recent design for a country house I walked around the site, thinking about the view of the lake, where I'd like to walk up a level or down, where I'd like to eat dinner, what I'd like to see when I woke up in the morning. Then I just started putting walls around it. When I do children's rooms it's the same kind of thing. I just get a feeling of how I think it would work, then I do it.

Two families live in the same line of the same building on Central Park West in New York. I designed children's rooms for both families in roughly the same area of each apartment. The first family wanted separate bedrooms for each of the two girls (see pages 54-56).

The second family offered to give up their generously large master bedroom for a smaller one if I could use the additional space to design something very unusual for their two boys. They were willing to let the boys have virtually their own quarters, quite separate from the rest of the apartment. I interpreted this as a challenge to provide special spaces for each of the two boys' major activities: playing, studying, and sleeping. There are two kinds of play space here. One is for quiet play such as reading and board games. Then there is one large space which both boys share for running trains and more active games. There's another space for sleep-over guests.

The boys had no trouble getting used to small, segregated spaces for different activities because the family lives on a boat in the summer. They're used to ladders and tight little corners. The boys are content to play here for hours, leaving the rest of the apartment to their parents.

One complete section of a Central Park West apartment, including what had been the master bedroom, was remodeled by architect Robert Rhodes to become self-contained quarters for two boys, Jason and Gregory. The complex contains two bedrooms, a small bathroom, a large play space, and a cozy sitting area for TV and listening to music.

The two overlapping bedrooms are separated from the main space by sliding doors with rounded cutouts. Hospital-type grab bars encourage the boys to slide the doors into the desired position or to play geometric games. The door cutouts have clear Plexiglas inserts and the circular portholes have colored Plexiglas panels that slide across those openings. Alternating colored stripes run through the vinyl-asbestos tile floor. A band of undercounter-type fluorescent fixtures runs along opposite walls about 30 inches below the ceiling. The rounded door provides access to a storage space for extra-large items. Hanging closets are provided elsewhere.

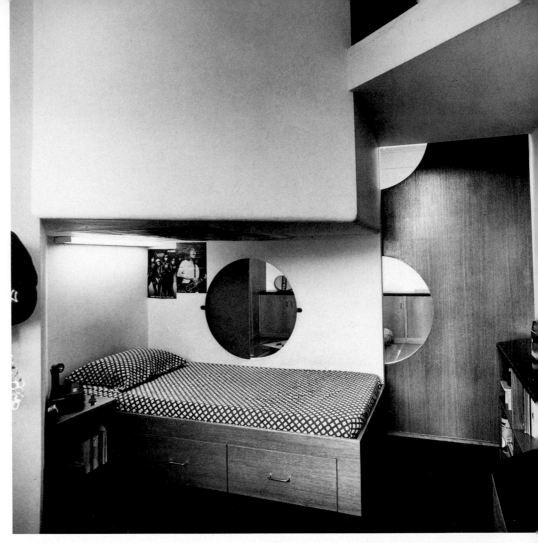

Both bedrooms and lofts are carpeted and each has a window desk and open shelves and drawers along the adjacent wall. The desk and adjacent surface have dark-brown Plexiglas tops, an unusual but practical use of this material. Gregory's loft is mainly for storage.

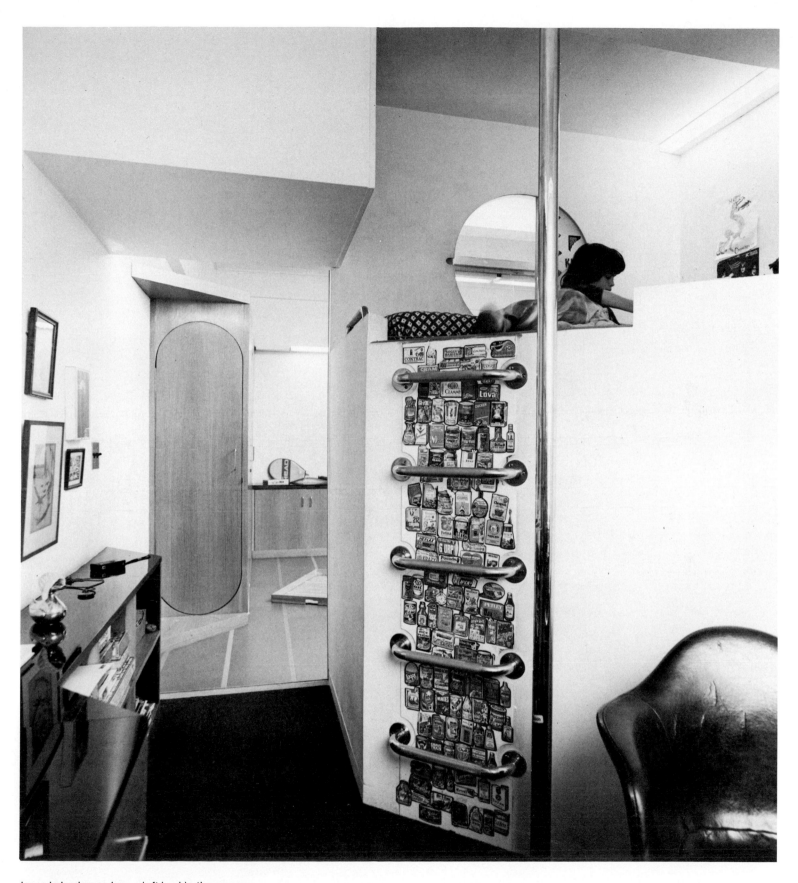

Jason's bedroom has a loft bed in the space that protrudes into the adjacent room. Again, institutional-type grab bars are used. There is a sturdy steel pole for rapid descent. A Plexiglas panel decorated with stickers prevents scuffing of the wall behind. Over the doorway at left there is additional storage.

Occupying similar space in the same apartment building as the remodeling shown in the preceding photos, this design, also by Robert Rhodes, for Lynn could hardly be more different. The nicely articulated, built-in unit is finished with white Formica, as is the panel of wall by the desk. Posters and notes may be taped to this panel without damage. The wall above the beds is covered with a light-camel-colored felt. Beneath the higher bed is a secret hideaway.

On the wall opposite, used like regular wallpaper, is this giant poster. Running a few inches onto the ceiling, the design almost completely camouflages the closet door in the center.

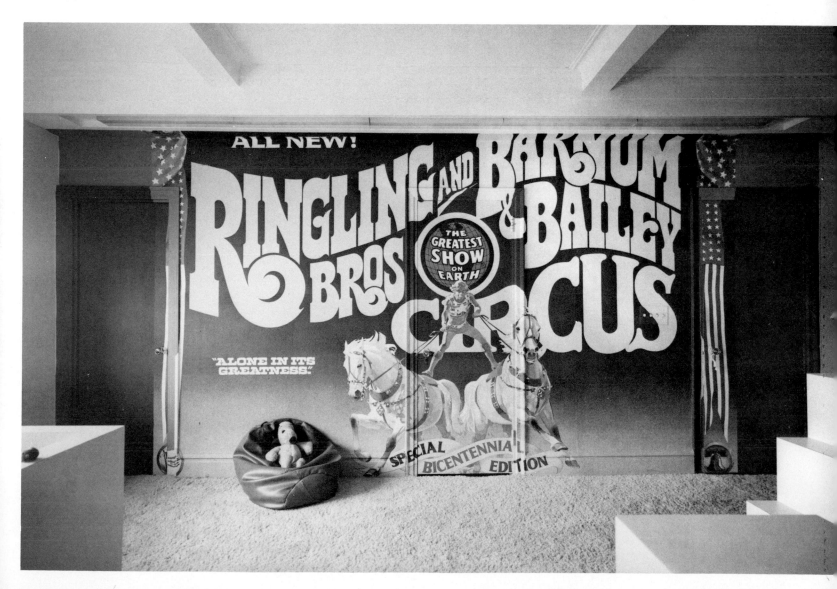

Tammy's room was converted from a maid's room and part of the adjacent dining area by architect Robert Rhodes. The surfaces are Formica and the wall behind the beds is covered with felt similar to that in her sister, Lynn's, room. Institutional grab bars are used as steps to the upper bed and also as drawer pulls. Open shelves flank the window on both sides. Tammy decorated her bulletin board herself. The python on the floor is a long snakelike pillow.

A freestanding seven-foot-high box provides unusual storage and preserves the spacious feeling and nice proportions of this high-ceilinged room designed by Barbara Simmons. The generous ceiling height permitted the addition of the airplanelike enclosure complete with escape chute. Rounded edges of corners and openings distinguish these added elements from the basic space.

Charles Gwathmey

I approach the design of a child's room very much as I do any other architectural problem, with consideration for what the person needs who will live in the space, what the possibilities are for use of the space, what the light is like, where the best view is . . . then I design it. Later on there are choices to be made regarding surfaces. They can be made of cork, Formica, tack-up, mirror—these are some of the possibilities. The child can participate in decisions of this kind. Working this way, I provide a room which is a framework for the way the child wants to live.

When I design a house, I am concerned less specifically with the personalities of the clients as a given in the program than I am with such factors as the possibilities of the site, the best approach to it, the requests in the program for accommodation. I see a house as a building that is made "specific" by the people who live there. Thus, if the program states that the teen-age boy is a hockey freak, I'll find a way for him to practice in his room. If he likes tennis, I might have one wall painted a dark color for him to hit against. But apart from that, I'll leave it to him to animate his own space.

In my family, the boys, Robbie and Eric, have rooms that are quite similar as to space and basic accommodation (see pages 46, 62). But the boys don't think of them as similar. They have the same furniture but they use the rooms in opposite ways. Robbie throws his football around in his room for hours. Eric plays music, or reads, or stands in the middle and hits a tennis ball against the colored wall. Robbie likes to set up all his things on his shelves and on his desk. When he throws the ball, everything comes down, but he doesn't mind, he likes to set them up again. He likes having his own pictures with colors that he enjoys, and so does Eric. In these ways each room reflects the personality of the boy who lives there.

I don't think you should feel as if you've walked through a sheer wall at the fun house when you go into the children's room. I think the space itself can override and be organized and still reflect the identity of the children in it.

In the apartment I did for another family, two of the children's rooms are similar, and a third is a different shape (see pages 59-61). All three rooms are designed with equivalent storage, sleeping, and play space. But the children were allowed to choose from four materials to be used in the surface of their rooms. One boy chose cork so he could hang up all his posters. His room looks nothing like his sister's, who chose mirror and a painted wall. The furniture disappears and what you are aware of is the contrast between the mirror and the colored wall as opposed to the cork and the posters in the boy's room. The children have succeeded in making their rooms very specific within a rather general framework.

I guess I approach all spaces in terms of the elements of the problem I have to solve. I think that's the strength of our buildings. They're specific in form but they get their form not from the personalities of people but because those people

The built-in furniture in this Gwathmey-Siegel room for skier Jill differs from her brother's only in the mirror that Jill chose to have over the bed, where Scott chose to put corkboard for his poster collection.

have four children, not one, and there's a view that way but not the other. It isn't important to me to know the clients very well. I'm not a voyeur. What my clients do or think in their houses is not my business.

I think "exclusive" design makes everything so specific that the user does not have options in his own mind to have dreams. Our spaces are calm and enduring. They are reinforced by issues that are going to exist no matter who is there: the sun rises, the light comes in, the trees change from season to season, it rains, it snows—this is what our spaces relate to. The solids and the voids are legitimate because they are there for reasons, and those reasons will not disappear. Beyond that, there is another level of design possibilities. On that level children can make the environments we design specifically theirs.

The architectural forms in a child's room designed by Charles Gwathmey are as clearly defined as those in any room of a Gwathmey-Siegel house. The shape of this room and of Jill's are the same and the built-in furniture is identical. But the rooms look different because of what the children have put into them.

Sportsman Scott enjoys the niche above his storage cabinets with a visiting friend. If the friend stays overnight, there is an extra bed that pulls out trundle-style from below the one shown. The vertical opening conveniently near the door of the room is ideal for storing such cumbersome sports equipment as hockey sticks and baseball bats.

In Charles Gwathmey's family, thirteen-year-old Eric likes to read, or play music, or hit a tennis ball against the pale-blue wall in his room. The furnishings in Eric's room are the same as those in his brother, Robbie's (see page 46), but Eric's choices of color for the wall, and the art to go on it, make the room look quite different.

This new interest in interiors by architects came about because there was no other kind of work. I used it, unconsciously perhaps, as a vehicle to discover a realm of spatial perception that I would not have reached nearly so fast any other way.

—CHARLES GWATHMEY

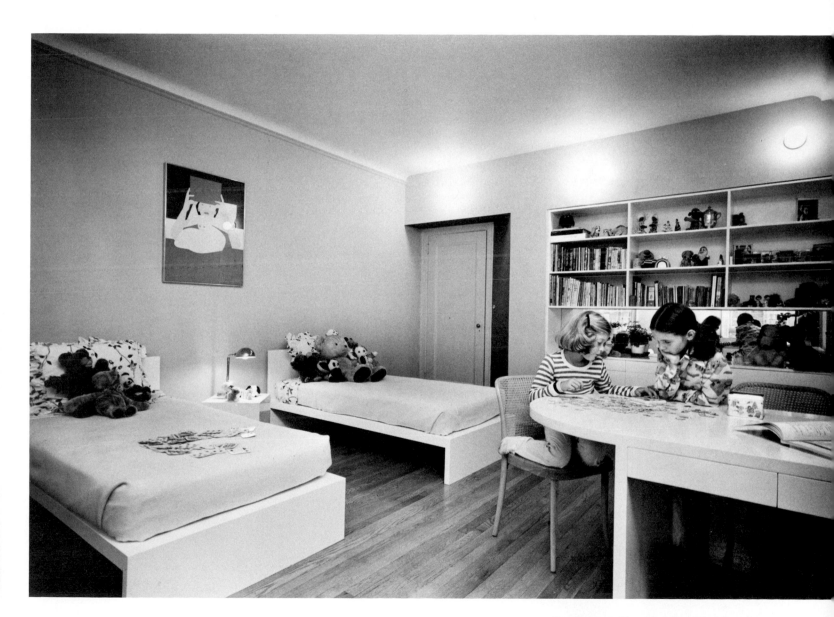

Courtney and her friend put their heads together to solve a puzzle in Courtney's room, designed by her father, Charles Gwathmey. The colored wall on the left, in an otherwise white room, provides a suitable background for the streamlined shapes and spaces. A strip of mirror at child's-eye level gives the impression of more space on the other side of the shelves.

Sharon Lee Ryder

Some of the clearest memories of my childhood are of all those times spent fanatically rearranging the furniture in the various rooms I inhabited in our rambling Victorian house, either because I had grown bored with the present arrangement or some new idea had clutched at my imagination, demanding to be realized. My mother was rather indulgent of this peculiar trait in her only child, not showing the least sign of surprise on discovering, one day, that I had moved all the furniture into the middle of the room, to afford myself easy access to everything from the commanding position of my bed. There was never a query as to what I was doing or, even, why. Somehow it was understood, perhaps with a certain relief, that I confined my creative binges to my own room and did not subject the rest of the household to my ever-changing whims.

These various places of habitation were very much my own domains, private retreats where I could ponder the inexplicability of adult behavior or plot revenge on my friends who had just set off in search of amusement without inviting me along. And there was always just the right place to be in my room, relative to my unpredictable states of mind: a window seat with vast views of the rolling lawn and arching elms for the times I was feeling particularly expansive and generous toward the world; or a nook into which I could crawl when my easily bruised ego was suffering from malnutrition and I felt I had no friends left.

There have been many different rooms over the years. Some, I recall with horror, were really rather ordinary, despite the best efforts of my imagination. But throughout this incomprehensible process of pushing, shoving, and rearranging, I grew up and, like the child who fantasizes about the day he will be able to eat all the ice cream he wants, I became an architect. . . .

The floor and platform surfaces of Douglas's room by Sharon Lee Ryder are covered with commercial carpeting made by the General Felt Company. The mattresses are wrapped in coarse blue Indian cotton from Fabrications, Inc. Above the desk is a partially enclosed private library, where Douglas can retreat when he wants to be alone. See also page 48.)

Hugh Hardy

The design of spaces for children requires respect as much as authority. It can be great fun if approached with humor and the understanding that all such places are temporary, because they must be changed as children grow.

Since their energy and imagination are almost boundless, children like rooms that are responsive to change, change that they produce themselves. They like a variety of spaces that they can use in different ways. It should also be remembered that they are smaller, and an adult-sized room can easily contain at least two layers of their activity.

Unlike adults, who use rooms basically for sedentary activities arranged within fixed furniture groupings, children take to the floor. Almost everything happens there, or ends up there. This is their natural turf, and its despoilment results in the ancient parental cry "Pick up your room!" This call for order comes from the parent, not the child, because adults see organization of clutter as a necessity. So, inevitably, a good design scheme for a child's room must include places to put things, places accessible and sensible enough to encourage order.

Children do organize things they prize: tools, baseball cards, comic books, or jewelry. When held in esteem, these talismans are lined up in neat rows, carefully organized in boxes, or painstakingly arranged for private delight and public display. Whatever the intended goal, interior design is itself an ordering process.

Color is important in a child's world. The difference between blue and yellow is as clear to youngsters as the cool discoveries of proportion are to adults. A rich and fearless use of color should be part of design for children right from the start.

Level changes in a child's room permit a variety of vantage points. Upper levels can become fortresses and ships; low levels become tunnels, houses, and secret hiding places. But there is no need to be specific about this. Children have such a visual imagination of their own that the efforts of adults to give rooms a "ship motif" or a "garden atmosphere" probably go by unnoticed. These are the artifices of the literal-minded "decorator," not the child.

Rooms for children should be places of transition, environments that are inevitably replaced if not forgotten. This ephemeral nature is their challenge and their joy.

Hugh Hardy's room for his son, Sebastian, shows how many elements of an earlier design (see page 73) can be retained while others are updated. Parts of the basic 2 by 4 frame of the first bed were saved when the family moved to a new apartment when Sebastian was six years old. The stylized cutout trees and the lower bed added in the new space make the unit look quite different. The unit is freestanding, permitting access to the built-in closets behind. As in the previous Hardy apartment, the floor area remains uncluttered for projects such as Sebastian's model railroad. The dark stripe on the right underscores a bookshelf (not shown) and unifies the room.

Children should be encouraged to participate in the making of their environments. They should help plan, design, draw, paint, and even hammer the nails. Otherwise they don't have a sense of the place being theirs. —MALCOLM HOLZMAN

Maxwell Holzman's bedroom is the handiwork of Malcolm Holzman & Son. The platform bed is raised to the ideal height for playing under and on. The ladders provide access to the bed and are marvelous just for climbing.

Alexandra Stoddard

For a child's place to be a growing, flexible environment, as little as possible should be fixed in one spot. The room should grow, change, and develop as the child does. The room should be designed for the child, not for the parents. It should reflect as much as possible the child's own ideas, interests, and feelings. It should be a place where you can let your child grow and expand in a supportive world. The room should fit the child and work for him.

The basic requirements are simple. Think of this room as a stage on which some props will stay and others will change. Plan the constants to last; for instance, you'll always have to have a place for the child to sleep, a place to store things such as clothes, art work, and paraphernalia. Free space for creative play, for friends, for books, for important activities, ranging from counting sea shells to having a slumber party. This one room should be flexible so that a child can live out each day in this one wonderful place—"My Room." (See page 47.)

From *A Child's Place* by Alexandra Stoddard.
Copyright © 1977 by Alexandra Stoddard.
Used by permission of Doubleday & Company, Inc.

A common problem in children's rooms is finding storage and display space for precious objects. Martin Rich solved this problem in eleven-year-old Emily's room by designing a series of units that runs the full length of the wall. The work surface even continues at right angles over the radiator by the window. Rich lowered the ceiling except for the central bay over Emily's bed, hiding beams and giving the space a more contemporary look. The contractor for this New York City room was Steve Milom.

We considered many different schemes for Emily's room—platforms, divisions in the room, a semicircular headboard. All of these seemed a little gimmicky. Things that are too gimmicky get old very quickly. What we finally decided on for Emily is a very functional space that she can grow in.
—MARTIN RICH

It was seven-year-old Sara's suggestion to include a movable ladder when Martin Rich designed a new room for her several years ago. The library ladder from Putnam Rolling Ladder Company in New York City permits ready access to the loft bed and otherwise out-of-reach cupboards, leaving ample space for a desk and counters below. Large red storage cubes, custom-made in wood, float around on casters and tuck neatly under the counters. A metal strip called a plug mold, with electrical outlets every 6 to 8 inches, provides an inexpensive alternative to a track-lighting system.

In this room designed by Alan Chimacoff of Chimacoff/Peterson, there is a place for everything in the Formica-finished, floor-to-ceiling cabinetry, which entirely covers one wall except for the windowed bed alcove. This is one of two similar rooms, each with its own exterior entrance, specifically planned to reduce traffic through the house.

"Why waste valuable floor space for beds?" said Hugh Hardy and his children Sebastian and Penelope. Using plywood and a ready-made ladder, Hardy made a duplex sleeping and playing space in a Greenwich Village room that is more vertical than horizontal. Open-topped storage boxes have casters for easy moving. Two small desks at the back are in a more private space.

The cushions make ideal furniture for kids. When Jason was very small, he pulled himself to a standing position on them. As soon as he could, he piled one on top of the other, gradually learning to climb from one level to the next without fear. He learned about hard surfaces in time, but his first falls were on soft, malleable objects that never hurt him. Now he sometimes kicks them if he feels aggressive, but he never draws or writes on the cushions. He has never put a mark on them. I think making our whole environment accessible to him has caused him to be not less, but more respectful of our things as well as his own. —SHEILA DE BRETTEVILLE

Jason de Bretteville and his friends amuse themselves for hours building imaginary environments with the De Brettevilles' Cohide-covered urethane cushions. One minute they are piling the lightweight yellow cushions high to make a skyscraper. Ten minutes later they've built a multilevel cave dwelling, or a tower, or a train. When Jason's building projects are over, the cushions are belted together again with bands of Cohide to form a comfortable seating arrangement for the grown-ups in this unusually airy Los Angeles house.

California architect Peter de Bretteville and his wife, Sheila, a graphic designer, feel that their whole house is as much their child's environment as it is theirs. Seven-year-old Jason has a small bedroom upstairs, but he plays mostly in the main living space of the house, not far from the grown-ups.

We want to combine in one room the functions of a living room, dining room, and kitchen. The idea is not to have a totally open plan but to have one level with a single major living space and a work space. Then, on a second level, we made closed cellular spaces quite separate from the larger ones below. These spaces, the bedrooms, are soft, cavelike places, as private as possible.   —PETER DE BRETTEVILLE

ADDING A ROOM

By the time a first child is eight or ten, there are often younger children in the family. Space may be getting tight as the family grows and the children become more active. This is a point at which families frequently look for a house in the suburbs, or for a bigger house. Or they may decide to add a room to their current living quarters to relieve the pressure.

Even if the family moves to the suburbs, it may not gain much space. Middle-income families cannot afford to buy, pay taxes on, or maintain as much space as they might have fifty years ago. Americans are learning to live in smaller spaces and like it. They have traded large bedrooms and separate dining rooms for dual-purpose spaces and family rooms.

Families who keep their city apartments often decide to have a weekend house in the country, somewhere beyond the suburbs. Some who find this possible are willing to endure more confined living quarters in the city. Because they have ample space to spread out in when they go to the country, their children may be content with small spaces of their own in the city that allow them simply to have privacy and a sense of separation from other members of the family.

For other families, the large house, like the large car, may still be possible and preferable to anything else. In some cases, children of two marriages may share such a house with one of their remarried parents for several months of the year. In these houses, attics and formerly neglected spaces will be divided up and made not only livable, but also appealing. Such renovations are frequently good examples of necessity being the mother of invention.

Amy Scott

The house where I spent my first fifteen years had three stories, a cellar with a central furnace we could roller-skate around, and a huge backyard with a section for gardens and grass, a worn part where we played ball, and a wild part with thick grasses and berry bushes that led to the woods. I first became conscious of these spaces when I was nine and playing at a friend's house. Her family lived on the second floor of a two-family house. It was so strange to me that she didn't go upstairs to bed, but just around the corner. I could even see her bedroom from the dining room!

Since my experience with city living began eight years ago, I have tried to remember different kinds of living spaces, how they compare and contrast with each other, and what they mean to children. It seems that one conspicuous difference between most city spaces and others is that in an apartment, the flow of many kinds of activity is limited: There is no simple connection between inside and outside. There is likely to be a long flight of stairs in between, and a door with two or three locks, or an elevator that isn't always there. Until a child is a certain age, he simply cannot go outside without an older person.

In most apartments there are no level changes. Functionally distinct areas are not architecturally distinct, as they usually are in houses with several stories. A child in a house spends a great deal of time first in mastering the process of going up and down stairs, and then simply galloping the route many times a day. In an apartment there is usually no difference in level between the public area—kitchen, living room, dining room—and the private part, the bedrooms, where each person has a place of his own and a child has somewhere to keep his treasures. A child in an apartment has fewer options. There are fewer kinds of passage between spaces, and fewer places to go. A child's room thus gains in importance as one particular space within the domestic structure. In designing children's rooms in the city I have tried to enrich spatially the apartment situation, within its physical and psychological limitations, to provide as many opportunities as possible for the kind of movement that occurs naturally in houses.

One of my first assignments was to convert a large dining room into two children's rooms for Jennifer, age seven, and Samantha, age three. The project required blocking off the original doorway, opening two new doors, and building a wall to make two separate spaces. In working on designs for play/sleeping lofts and the necessary storage, I realized that these units could *be* the dividing wall. Details in the shaping of these functional units came from my desire to create different kinds of spaces within each of these fairly small rooms, making possible different kinds of activity related to the shapes of the units. It was decided that each room would have a second level, with a ladder as a means of access. Here would be the possibility of climbing; here is up and down. Under part of the loft is a small playhouse cubbyhole. The ladder, with a piano hinge and casters, is its door. There is motion in the structure itself as the ladder-door is opened and closed. Another kind of activity is suggested by the cubbyhole: going into, coming out.

The window in the "head" wall between the girls' rooms makes possible verbal and visual communication and also provides an alternative to the more conventional doorway as a means of entering a room. This third kind of activity might be labeled "passing through."

In the rooms for Lyris and Jennifer I designed a two-way bookcase. Some of the shelves are for the blue room and some are for the yellow room. The back of the yellow shelves appears in the blue room as a blank face, slightly recessed. The reverse is true in the yellow room. In this unit I saw a way of connecting the two rooms, making an optional means of passage, with an element of mystery and surprise. One section of the bookcase appears in each room as a blank face, but is actually a door. By using touch catches on them, there is no doorknob to spill the secret, and each catch can be operated only from the front. Each child's own door can be opened, but to get through the second door into the other room, the neighbor must open the way. Thus four cubic feet of possible shelf space has been exchanged for an opening and closing activity, a place to go and a way to get there.

Although these rooms are designed for young children, they are not scaled down in any way. I have chosen as a primary guideline not the size of the children, but their high level of energy and curiosity. Anyone with similar liveliness, even a grown-up, can move up and down, in, around, and through all these structures.

Where once there was a single large bedroom, Amy Scott made two fascinating rooms for Lyris, shown here with her brother, and Jennifer. In Lyris's blue-and-white room, a box with an oval opening appears on the other side of the wall as Jennifer's loft bed with shelves near the floor.

Open shelves forming box shapes neatly frame Jennifer's favorite objects, books, and records. Her clothes are tucked away in compartments behind closed doors.

Amy Scott designed a secret pass-through from one sister's room to the other. The doors at either end can be opened only with the cooperation of the child on the other side.

Another example of compartmentalized storage is this wall of open shelves designed by Ivan Chermayeff for his daughter Catherine. The shelves are on tracks so they can be moved up or down to make an opening of the desired size. The neat and methodical arrangements are all by Catherine and include such treasures as a lock of one of the Beatles' hair.

Barbara Ross
& Barbara Schwartz
Dexter Design, Inc.

Whether we design for older children, or children the age of Adam, four, and Gaby, one, we try to think of all the phases of change and development the child will go through in that room. For most families, a child's room is most successful if it is designed for change right from the start, instead of being so perfect for the child at one stage that it looks babyish and inappropriate later on.

A specific design problem that confronted us in a children's room was to divide one large space into four separate areas, each with a particular function. Adam and Gaby each need their own bedrooms. We planned, in addition, an area in the middle that can serve as a place for their older sister, Jeannie, to sleep when she comes to stay on school vacations. This is a place for the housekeeper to sleep, too, when the parents are away for a few days. When it's not being used as a sleeping space, it's a cozy place to curl up and read, to listen to a record or watch TV. Then there is the larger open area where the children can play actively. Along the sides, special compartments have been designed for storage of bicycles, winter clothes, skis, and other cumbersome equipment which is so hard to find a place for in a New York apartment. All the spaces are distinct from each other, yet because of the clerestory space at the top of each room, they all share good lighting and ventilation. (See pages 102-103.)

We used Levolor blinds as a divider above the plywood partitions between the two bedrooms. The children keep the blinds open now, but as they grow older and privacy is more important to them, the blinds can be closed. The Levolor blinds help to isolate the occasional-sleeping space, too. If a baby-sitter or another adult is spending the night there, the light can be turned on over the bed for reading and when the blinds are closed, it will not disturb the children.

At the entrance to each child's bedroom there are closets with lots of room to hang things. Because of the placement of storage for clothes here, this space at the entrance to the room becomes a dressing room for the child. It also serves as a transition space between the door to the room and the major area of the room where the bunks and desk are.

We used every spare inch for storage. Above every cabinet, under every bed, inside of or behind almost every structural element there is a place to put something. That was, along with separation of spaces, the outstanding achievement of the room. We were also concerned with making it pretty. We chose colors and fabrics that reflect the taste and interests of the children now. That part can change as they grow older.

Joy Wulke created a fabric environment of clouds and flowers in the middle seating area. This provides a marvelous background for the children's imaginations as they lose themselves in the stories that they read or listen to in this part of the room. As they grow older, the clouds and flowers may be replaced by something more sophisticated, more monochromatic. The room may take on a more serious aspect with different furniture and accessories, but the structural basis of the space is there. It can change its appearance without major renovation.

In Adam's first nursery, Alan Buchsbaum and
Michael Wolfe used color to define the
perimeters of a very large room. The yellow
wall stripes are broken up into measured
lengths to show the comparison between feet
and meters.

Adam's later private quarters by Dexter
Design, Inc., are small but well equipped with
storage space, work surface, and a place for
a visiting friend to sleep. His bunk bed is from
The Workbench in New York City. The quilts
are from Groundworks. The wall next to the
built-in Formica cabinets has a metal surface
made by Alliance Wall that can be used as a
magnetic bulletin board. It can be drawn or
painted on, and then wiped clean.

Gaby is caught unawares as she and her doll watch television in the part of the children's play space she shares with her brother Adam. Every nook and cranny is used for one sort of storage or another; no space is wasted. The TV wall in this shared space has built-in units by Interlubke from International Contract Furniture in New York. The lamps are from Luxo Lamp Corporation. The wall hanging is part of the soft-sculpture environment created by Joy Wulke of Fiber Works.

Jim Swan

A few months before our first child was born, Sara and I moved to the top floor of a Victorian house in Greenwich Village. Certain structural changes had to be made in the space because the things that were there had rotted or were poorly placed. What we had when we finished our process of renovation was one major space with no partitions except those to separate the kitchen and bathroom, and one closet that we built as a kind of spatial modulator.

Our son, Christopher, started life in one corner of this wide-open space. There was plenty of room for his crib and the few things he required. As he grew older and we felt the need for more privacy, walls started to spring up. As we made these walls, we thought it was important to make them acceptable to the people who would live with them. We tried to think ahead to all possible uses of our spaces in the future. When Erin, our daughter, came along, it seemed appropriate that she should have her own space, just as the rest of us did. So we extended the balcony, to make a bedroom for ourselves, and made a bedroom for her where we had formerly slept. So then Erin and Christopher each had their own rooms in opposite corners of the apartment, with a combined play area in between.

The major feature of Christopher's room is his aerie, or what he calls his "combine." Just before this part of his bedroom was built, we had visited some relatives on a farm in Maryland. They had an enormous harvesting combine which we all went up into. The cab of this machine was at least twenty feet above the ground. It made quite an impression on Christopher. His combine has recently doubled as a pirate ship, a castle—it changes with Christopher's mood and imagination. Another advantage of the combine from Christopher's point of view is that it is a place where grown-ups can't go, or at least not without being very uncomfortable. We only venture up there in cases of dire necessity.

Once the rooms were there, it was evident that they were going to be small, but we were willing to accept that. The subsequent decisions then had to be made about how furniture was going to be dispersed and storage space provided. What we decided to do was combine all the accouterments for living—shelves for toys, drawers and hanging space for clothes, bed—in one unit. In this way we left the walls free but made circulation space rather tight. The children, being small, don't mind this. They like to have spaces that are identifiably theirs, to control in whatever ways appeal to them.

Years ago, when I was younger and maxims appealed to me, I used to say that in various ways it is good to maximize the individual's possibilities of choice, without inhibiting the choices of other individuals. If you can do this in an environment, many conflicts and petty squabbles can be avoided. We've designed this apartment so that each of us has a place to be an individual with all the rights that that implies, while still sharing companionship and living space with other members of the family.

To survey his domain, Christopher can climb by built-in ladder to his watchtower above his bed, 5½ feet from the floor. An orange-juice box on a pulley transports toys to the watchtower. The unit is a copyrighted design by architect James Swan. Furniture designs by James Swan, represented by Pivot Design Services, Inc., New York City.

Christopher's bed-storage "aerie" also forms an island under the eaves at one end of the Swans' Greenwich Village apartment. More toys sit neatly on the open shelves at the rounded corner. On the right is a clothes closet with doors hung on piano hinges. The standard-size bed is like a peninsula stretching from the island-tower back into Christopher's space.

From Erin's room, we look across the top
floor of the Swan house, past the play-storage
area, to Christopher's room.

In a Manhattan apartment, artist-carpenter Amy Scott converted a dining room into two bedrooms for Samantha, age three, and Jennifer, seven, by making two 13-foot-long spaces that are mirror images of each other. She divided the original space with one continuous bed-storage wall. Where one part of the wall is indented for a bed, the unit on the other side offers a smooth facade with shelves and storage space below. The opposing sleeping space can be glimpsed in the photograph through the 20-inch-square opening at the foot of the bed. The yellow panels hanging on the wall fit into grooves on either side of this opening for either complete (solid panel) or partial (heart-shaped panel) privacy. The ladder to the sleeping loft swivels on a piano hinge so Samantha can use the space below her bed for a "carriage house."

Preserving both light and ventilation for each space, Amy Scott devised and built this complex divider for the awkward room with adjacent corner windows. Open shelves and enclosed storage are exactly duplicated for each child's space.

Judith York Newman

The primary considerations in designing for children are the concepts of storage, scale, and self.

Storage is the simplest to define. It means having a room that gives its keeper the ability to organize with ease. I've found the best excuse a child can have not to put something away is that there is no place to put it. When it's necessary to push, cram, and maneuver, it is certain that the temptation will be to leave everything out. Storage can be fun and, therefore, an incentive to neatness. One solution is to build a raised floor so that hinged trapdoors provide access to large compartmented recesses below. Another solution is to recycle old wooden file drawers by incorporating them as a unit under a new counter. These provide ample drawers for the bulky toys of a young child who later may want to fill them with a comic-book collection or other precious treasures.

The need for scale in a child's space can be defined as the need for the right place of the right shape and of the right size. To a child, this could be a corner or an empty space over a closet. Any kind of enclosure can give a feeling of seclusion or the excitement of a perch. This could involve a change in level. Or it might be a surface that is a desk and extends to become a platform or a sleeping level. Children seem to gravitate toward small private spaces, especially for sleeping. An upper bunk is often high on a child's priority list. It's a good choice because it makes it possible to have an extra bed or even a cozy desk area below the bunk.

A child's sense of self springs from his relationship to his environment as he plays, sleeps, dresses, studies, relaxes there. This sense can be heightened by having places for plants, pets, books, or particular activities. I asked my eleven-year-old son what he likes about his room. He zeroed in on its generous size. It is big, and because everything is built in, it appears bigger. His second favorite feature in this room is the large sink. It is stainless steel, kitchen variety, and he uses it to wash, conduct assorted experiments, and care for his gerbils. He also likes the different forms of privacy in his room. His upper bunk, where he chooses to sleep, has a wide shade that rolls down to block out any view. His desk is nestled behind a freestanding closet and the whole room is closed off by door-size panels which slide on an overhead track. His idea of the most super possible room would include his own telephone (preferably a videophone) and a whole wall with built-in electronic games. His sister is less demanding. She, at seven years old, seems to appreciate more than anything else the purple and orange colors in her room and the teak of her trundle bed. Is that because she is a girl? Or because she's still only seven years old?

David Hicks's room for his son in their country house shows how a small attic space can be made cozy and inviting. The striped sheet-fabric wall covering designed by Hicks for J. P. Stevens emphasizes the unusual contours of the ceiling. The bed does double duty as a sofa during the day.

MMcG.: *Barbara, what do you think is the most important aspect of a child's environment?*

BARBARA ROWE *(mother of Chris): I think it should be both utilitarian and comfortable.*

MMcG.: *And you, Chris?*

CHRIS *(age fifteen): Privacy. That's most important. I need a place to be alone and not be bothered . . . a place where I can keep my things the way I want to keep them.*

MMcG.: *How organized do you like to be?*

CHRIS: *Certain things I keep in special places. Other things I put aside and never use, but I like to know they're there.*

Judith York Newman is an architect who specializes in the renovation of New York brownstones. In a house only 18 feet wide, she managed to make every inch count in two children's rooms formed by dividing the space at the rear of the house into narrow, interlocking rooms with one window each.

Though Christopher's room is small—only 8 by 16 feet—he likes the compact spaces where he can work and relax alone. His high bed gives him added privacy.

The approach to Gabriella's room is via a short corridor from the hall into the space on the other side of the wall she shares with Christopher. Ms. Newman has designed a closet made of oak that looks just right in a house where wood and exposed brick are major features.

Though the rooms are very contemporary, many of the furnishings reflect the age of the house. The quilt on Annie's bed, for example, came with the house when the Robinsons bought it.

Two of the three children's rooms connect directly with one another and share a small separate hall with Annie's corner room. Below the clerestory, opposite the windows, each room has a natural-finish redwood storage element, a nice contrast with the white plaster walls. The painting near the door is by Thomas Holland.

A giant keyhole frames the bedroom of architect James Rossant's daughter Marianne, on the top floor of the Federal Period house in SoHo. The room also serves as a living room for Marianne's two sisters when she is away at college.

Next page:
This remodeling provides complete, self-contained children's quarters, separate from the rest of the apartment. Converted from a large single space (see page 84), this is now a living-playing area with two small bedrooms behind. The transformation by Barbara Ross and Barbara Schwartz of Dexter Design, Inc., provides Adam with the privacy he now wants (see page 85) and gives Gaby, his younger sister, her own room—glimpsed through the door on the left. By keeping the partitions low, the designers have allowed light and ventilation to penetrate from the window wall beyond into all parts of the room. The central seating area, with its soft-sculpture environment by Joy Wulke of Fiber Works, doubles as a mini guest room that can be enclosed by Levolor blinds. More blinds control the clerestory light. The carpet is made by Burlington with fiber by Allied Chemical. Simpson Timber Co. APA grade-trademarked plywood; Anso = X nylon carpet by Burlington House.

Supergraphics designed by Alan Buchsbaum in dreamlike shapes enliven a space that was once an ordinary room. Architect Melvin Smith made it work for two little girls who wanted to have separate rooms but like to play together. The tricolor stripe moves in various configurations around the walls and moldings and across the door that slides between the girls' rooms.

Alan Buchsbaum

Humor, fantasy, bright bold color, nonconstrictive forms, and chaos—these are the words that describe my idea of a child's room. I suppose there are neat children, but I've yet to meet one. Children's rooms that are strong in design look good all the time. In fact, mess only adds to their gestalt. A preciously designed room, too perfect to touch, seems to me a difficult place for a child to grow up. The chaos added by the child makes it his or her private territory, a refuge from the adult world.

I use a child's expressed needs or preferences as a departure point for design. One little girl needed a blackboard for her graffiti and pinup space for her drawings. Her play-space requirement was fulfilled by folding the beds up into the wall (see page 167). A teen-age girl wanted a canopy bed (see page 158). Two sisters needed one room divided into two for their privacy, but they wanted some common space. A big sliding door satisfied that demand (see page 104).

In each of the rooms color and form were used in different ways. The room on page 104 has dreamlike shapes that flow from one room to the other. The forms disrupt the space and make what is essentially a small room into an infinite one. The room on page 84 is very large and color is used to reinforce the room's perimeter, which contains all the colorful objects. The wall stripes are broken up into measured distances to indicate the comparison between feet and meters. The room on pages 167-168 kept the pattern and color below 6 feet 8 inches to scale the room to a child's point of view. The wall graphics are created with paint, birch boards, and wallpaper. The room on page 158 has a fantasy leaf-pattern wall fabric that tends to disintegrate the enclosure of the walls. The Formica room on page 113 was part of a display in which an environment of a sports-minded child was depicted by using blowups of newspaper photographs of baseball players.

Paint is the primary material in many of these designs, since it is the most inexpensive and flexible tool for transforming space. As a child's requirements change, so can the room.

In this display for Formica, architect Alan Buchsbaum, in collaboration with Elizabeth Martin and Stephen Tilly, shows how blowups of newspaper photographs can be used to decorate a sports-minded boy's room. The furniture grouping shown in the photograph could be built as a freestanding unit with another bed, and a different decorative scheme, on the other side of the partition.

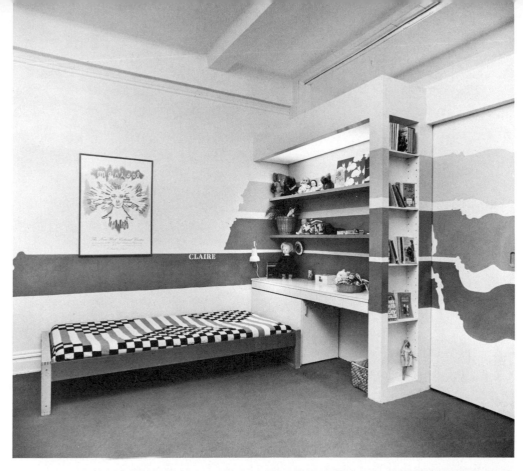

The cabinet beneath Claire's desk makes a handy hiding place for her pillow during the day. The glazed panel near the ceiling admits daylight to the inner room even when the sliding door is closed. (See also page 104.)

Leslie Armstrong

Moo and Nino's tiny bedrooms and playroom are located in the rear of the top floor of a 15-foot-wide New York City brownstone which was renovated in 1967. Originally there were two 6½-by-13-foot bedrooms plus random closets and shelving in this area. They resembled corridors, with a window at one end and a washstand at the other. When the area was cleared out, what remained was an almost square room. This was then divided into three smaller but better-proportioned spaces: the two 6½-foot-wide kids' rooms against the window wall, and an interior skylighted playroom, 6 by 13½ feet, with a full-width closet for both kids at one end and modular units at the other.

Little was added at the outset in the way of furniture, until Moo turned into a rambunctious five-year-old, demanding things to climb over, swing on, hide under. At this point a sleeping loft was built four feet above the floor across the door of her room. While grown-ups had to duck to enter her abode, she could sail in and out as she pleased. In the meantime, the cast of characters changed in the other space. The original occupant, Moo's half-brother, Lafcadio, then twelve, had outgrown the confines of such a small space, and even if he hadn't, he was being bumped out by the new baby, Nino. Once again, the crib and diaper table emerged.

Recently it became clear that Moo needed a more conventional bedroom setup. She needed a desk, some bookshelves, and proper storage space for her belongings. Nino was out of diapers and had his own increased storage requirements. Plus, the kids needed an additional place to house an overnight guest. Thus the loft in Moo's room came down and was recut to fit at standard height at the end of the playroom. Storage drawers were installed below. The two modular shelf units were placed in each kid's room. The trundle bed originally acquired for her room was returned from the cellar, new bedspreads were bought, and the place was painted up like mad. But how long it will be before the next change is anybody's guess.

Orange on yellow for Moo and pale green on blue for Nino mark the latest stage in the metamorphosis of these rooms by architect-mother Leslie Armstrong in her narrow New York brownstone. The sofa in the playroom was once a loft bed. Modular units that started out in the playroom have been separated and put in each of the tiny bedrooms.

Brothers, close in age, spend many hours together, but they value their privacy, too. In architect David Specter's house, when Matthew or Evan feels the need to be alone, a simple sliding partition separates the two rooms. Other times, especially when the boys have guests, the rooms open up to make ample space for games and other activities.

DOING THE MOST WITH THE LEAST

If parents do not build an addition to their house as the family grows, or if they are committed to a city apartment, one of the younger members may decide to commandeer any small space, just to have a place of his own. That space may not have been intended as a bedroom, or it may be that classic space known as the maid's room still found in city apartments of late-nineteenth-century vintage. An adult may see this space as nothing more than a glory hole, a storage room. A child contemplating a room of his own sees it with entirely different eyes.

It sometimes comes as a surprise to parents who like large, spacious rooms that their children prefer small, cozy spaces where they have a sense of being enclosed in their own private world. With some help from adults, small enclosed spaces need not lack any of the amenities that make life comfortable for a child. A 7-by-10-foot room can accommodate a giant Erector set with built-in loft bed and storage. It can be an audiovisual center with a library, bed, desk, and space to spare. The problem of dealing with a strangely shaped room with minimal space to put anything is not a problem at all when a good designer and an enthusiastic child apply themselves to it.

Sometimes children in a family choose to share a small room rather than be separated. The privacy of each child can be protected by dividers that partly separate each space. Or it can be done with platforms to make changes in level designating one area as different from another. Astute designers can show you that all these things are possible.

George Cody

In his early environment a child learns a great deal about what pleases his parents. He gains a sense of what objects they enjoy and what their values are in terms of privacy, space, and how to use space. How does your child learn these things, and how can you be sure he will respond positively to your "messages" about the environment he shares with you? Start with what is important to you. Think how you will share it with your small friend; then consider the special features that make it easier for you to live together and at the same time allow independence for you both.

In our house we do not believe in one all-purpose space such as the so-called family room. Although we spend a lot of time together as a family, possibly more than most families do, we think there should be different rooms for different activities: Cook in the kitchen. Sleep in the bedrooms (they don't need to be very big). Play where the block city doesn't topple when a parent demands a clear path. Read and talk to each other in the living room.

The living room is where the child discovers the spirit of his family. It should be an appealing place with comfortable furniture and a fireplace or other focus. Provide a cabinet to store a few special toys and games. Here is where two can play checkers while another reads, perhaps later falling into a conversation about what happened at school or how a checkerboard is made. If there is a bookcase, let the children have the bottom shelf. If you subscribe to magazines, make sure there are some that the children like tucked in with yours. Share in some of the fantasy of play in the living room. You may be surprised at the lasting decorative quality of a dollhouse in the living room; even an electric train track layout is tolerable there for a while. Watch it sprout a station, a bridge, a tunnel, a spur over books and blocks. A large living room offers more for everyone than large bedrooms. Making children welcome there gives them a feeling of equality in the family.

The whole second floor of our house is the children's floor. To arrive there, they ascend a winding stair. The suggestion of turrets and castles changes the feeling above from communal rooms to that of private chambers. All three children like having their bedrooms out of the community part of the house. They receive less critical interference from parents, a status they have enjoyed since they first moved into their rooms seven years ago at ages five, seven, and nine.

When a new interest dims yesterday's dream, our children's cast-off playthings are carefully stored in a private attic. This attic is a three-foot-wide space along the outside walls. The three-foot width was required by building setback regulations. The attic averages three feet high and is continuous between the rooms. Not only is it a valuable storeroom, but the darkened space is the perfect setting for involved games of mystery and adventure.

Separate from our house, its arbors, walks, and garden, is an eight-foot-wide side yard by the garage which the children call the CP, for Children's Paradise. Here they have always been free to dig holes, make roads and lakes (mud wallows), plant vegetables, and build things. Wood boxes, boards, rags, odd lengths of pipe, and pieces of metal are the raw materials to make a fort, a pirate ship, a tank, a submarine, or a playhouse. One of these constructions at the peak of its use may look like a dangerous mess that needs to be cleaned up. To the children it is a fantasy made real, an idea from their own heads that they can see and feel and make work. Eventually the image fades and the parts are restacked, awaiting a new challenge and the right mood to make something else happen.

When we planned our children's rooms and the other spaces our children use, maintenance was not our primary consideration. We care about quality and finish, so they have learned to care about quality and finish. A child's room should not be planned for an uncoordinated ruffian. "Childproof" is a dangerous concept, a little like "escapeproof" and "ratproof." Care for the things they live with has to be the children's responsibility, not that of some manufacturer. Pink-and-frilly for girls, blue-and-serviceable for boys are silly, contrived notions about things designed for children. Girls and boys are alike in that they want to be in places that are designed with honesty and sensitivity to their interests and needs.

A plywood elephant with a bed in his tummy, a hippopotamus to swallow soiled garments, may illustrate a circus theme, but they are architectural baby talk—a hurdle to a child's true perception of his environment. A child's first speech is baby talk. If your response is baby talk, it will be a long time before he knows his own language.

The Codys like to be together in their living room. While one member of the family repairs a broken toy, others play a game, or read, or talk. But there are times when everyone likes to be alone. The children's compact, cozy bedrooms are perfect for this.

From the top of the stairs on "the children's floor," one sees, as if from a medieval turret, the family living room below. The antique toys are from architect George Cody's valuable collection. They are there for grown-ups as well as children to enjoy.

119

Though the largest of the children's bedrooms in the Cody house is only 8½ by 13 feet, each one is well equipped. Every room has a five-foot-wide wardrobe in which there are built-in drawers with an oversized drawer at the bottom for shoes. The clothespole has three socket positions—symbols for the parents of passing time. The small washbasin and mirror relieve the pressure on the single upstairs bathroom.

The Cody boy's top bunk makes an excellent play table. The shelves in the cabinet at one end contain the electronic controls for a complete transportation system. The plywood landscape that supports this system is painted with roads and rivers. The giant bulletin board along the wall at the right is a panel of cane fiberboard ½ inch thick, painted with a coat of white primer.

The opening below the window provides access to an under-roof passage three feet wide and approximately three feet high which connects the Cody children's bedrooms. Much used when the children were younger, it now functions mainly as storage space. The inside of the door to this attic is a handy place to put the colorful stickers that many adults find annoying elsewhere.

121

The Harpers spend most of their leisure time together in a house that is designed to be shared. In addition, the Harper children have acres of outdoor space to explore when weather permits. The time they spend in their rooms is quiet time, mainly spent reading, doing homework, or just enjoying solitude.

Ian's room is 9 feet wide by 11⅓ feet high. It has no furniture other than the bed and the shelves over it. The drawers of the storage "tower" step upward following the profile of the steep stair behind which leads to Ian's crow's nest, a favorite spot, scaled just for a child.

The shelf supports in both Ian's and Mary Alice's rooms are the same. Contemporary renditions of the symbols for Comedy and Tragedy, one face is painted green, the other red.

We think of our whole house as an environment for children. We've designed it to be open enough for them to do whatever they like.

Where we live, there is plenty of space out-of-doors for running around, so we do not feel it is necessary for the children to have large bedrooms. We do think it is important for the children to have places to be by themselves, especially during the winter when it is too cold to go outside. And they need places to store the multitude of treasures they collect.

Our children's rooms are designed to serve these purposes, and, with their double levels, to provide opportunities for the children to imagine themselves in any number of places and situations.
—PATRICIA & ROBERT HARPER

Mary Alice's crow's nest is smaller than Ian's but just as cozy and her room is just as colorful as Ian's. The children helped choose the colors for their rooms: Mary Alice's bed is red with purple knobs on the storage drawers. Her blanket and carpet are bright green.

"All you really need in a bedroom is a bed, a desk, and a place to spread out," says ten-year-old Dago Dimster, suggesting that, in California, boys who play soccer and ride bikes most of the day don't need the same kind of interior space as a city child who spends little time out-of-doors. The blue-and-yellow bed-storage units in Dago and Don's room were a family project: designed by Frank and Dagmar Dimster, they were painted by Mr. Dimster's mother, with help from the boys. The modular units can be easily rearranged with changing requirements.

Martin Rich

I have two primary considerations in designing for children: (1) the needs and interests of the child, and (2) the spatial/scale definition within the room. These spatial considerations become especially important in very small rooms where the dimensional limits become the controlling factor.

The pattern that I have developed in designing rooms for children begins with my talking with both the child and the parents. While the parents have information about the child's needs, the child can usually provide the important clue that will give the room its special quality—what he or she feels is *missing* from the current environment. For example, one seven-year-old girl told me she spent a lot of time reading on the top shelf of her parents' closet. She really felt comfortable in that private space. I used this as a central idea in designing a reading loft in a room about 7 by 11 feet. She has used this loft in much the same way as she once used her parents' closet.

In all the rooms I've designed I have tried to make several distinct and different spaces within the room itself, spaces that can take on different characteristics—one might be more private, another more functional, another more public. I think the child should have a sense of being able to choose what to do, where to be, even in a very small room. In small rooms, it helps to make some miniaturized spaces or elements to create the illusion that the room is larger than it actually is. By reducing the scale of certain things, other things seem larger in contrast.

Usually, when I have arrived at a clear idea of a solution to a design problem, I do a three-dimensional model. Everyone in the family can examine it closely and see the relationship of its parts. The children can understand the design right away, and the model becomes their tool to discuss the details of the room with much more ease than is possible with a drawing.

Children, in their own ways, try to find special and personal places for themselves—tree houses, attic spaces, little huts in the backyard. Designers are only now beginning to recognize this. A child may demonstrate this need to create a place of his own (as I remember doing as a child) by putting cartons together in different configurations, or he may find one of a thousand other ways of telling us that it is important to have a sense of identification with the spaces he or she lives and plays in.

A sliding library ladder, custom-made with Putnam Rolling Ladder Company hardware, puts otherwise inaccessible objects within reach of the young teen-ager who lives in this room. A former maid's room next to the kitchen in a Manhattan apartment, the room, designed by Martin Rich, is only 7 by 11 feet. Plastic dishpans used as storage bins and Marimekko fabric on the bed add all the color this small space needs. The contractor-cabinetmaker for the room was Steve Milom.

Marion and Laura would rather climb to their playing space than have it on the same level as the bed. Sliding doors below the loft space conceal vertical and horizontal storage space. There are more deep drawers next to the bathroom entrance. Steve Milom was the contractor-cabinetmaker for this room designed by Martin Rich.

Martin Rich converted this pocket-sized room, 7 by 11 feet, into a multipurpose space. Under the play loft, at the left is a closet and beyond the desk on the right are drawers with open shelving above. The folding doors lead to a tiny bathroom. Laura and her sister Marion, whose room this is, are seen playing in the loft. The contractor-cabinetmaker for this work was Steve Milom.

129

Architect Rosemary Songer remodeled this 13-by-16-foot room for two young sisters in a New York condominium. The desk in the foreground is separated from a second work area (see pages 138-139) by the curved elements and drawers at the right. The high cabinets permitted by the ample 9½-foot ceiling height incorporate strip lighting and enclose one side of the upper bed. On the right is a mirror seen also in page 137. Through the opening, Karen is seen at a third desk, chatting with her sister, Jennifer. All surfaces are covered with a plastic laminate for easy maintenance. Cabinetwork by Sergio Mitnik.

"In this apartment," said the designer, Robert Stern, "we had the special problem of dividing one room for two girls so that each girl would feel that her part of the room had its own identity, but that neither girl had more than her sister—more bookshelves, more space, more anything. We divided the room down the center, using a mirror-image plan, with color as a means of defining each girl's space. As they were not going to have two radios, two phonographs, two TV's, there is a certain part of the wall which both girls share; they can reach through it. The rest of the wall is solid, clearly marking off each girl's territory."

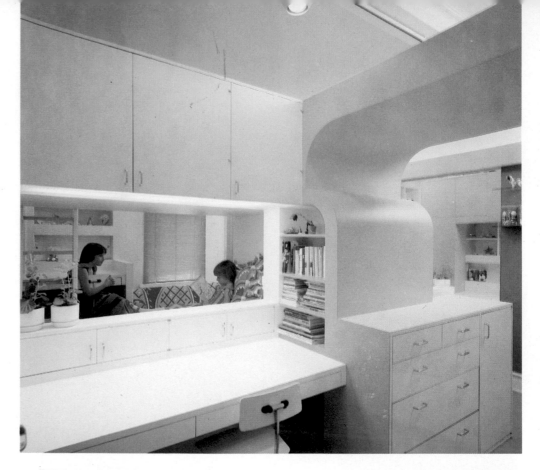

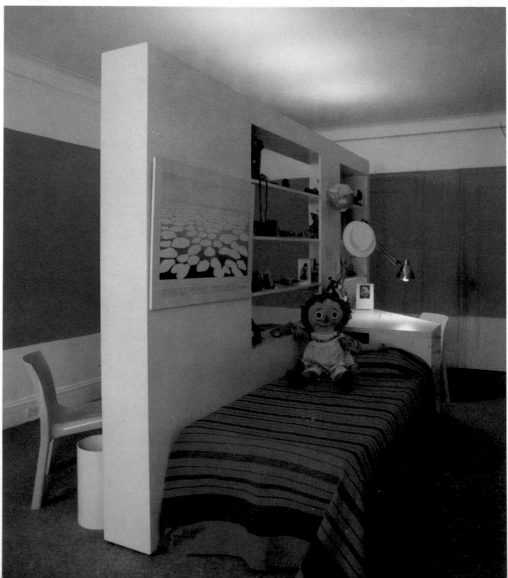

You can make a room for a child, with space for an overnight guest, that costs less than $200 to build, not counting the minor expense of three small chests of drawers. This former maid's room, converted by architect John Copelin into a room for his daughter, Stephanie, shows what can be done with simple framing and a few cans of red and yellow paint.

Thomas Rossant's desk and bed are both supported by scaffolding made from ¾-inch steel pipe with Speed-Rail joints that are easily adjustable in height. The pipe is readily available in various lengths and sizes from industrial-supply or large hardware stores and is used here as it comes, unpainted.

Though Thomas Rossant's room is only 7 by 10 feet, he has more floor space than his friends with larger rooms. The loft bed built by his father, James Rossant, leaves walls free for Thomas's collection of hats and decorative memorabilia.

Developed by Conklin and Rossant with the A. G. Hollaender Company, Cincinnati, Ohio, this Speed-Rail and complementary-components system provides a desk, storage receptacle, and/or bed platform. The pipe has cast-aluminum-alloy joints so that rods can be made to cross each other at different angles. Only an allen wrench is required to assemble the system. There is a powder epoxy finish on the joints and enamel on the ¾-inch-diameter aluminum pipes.

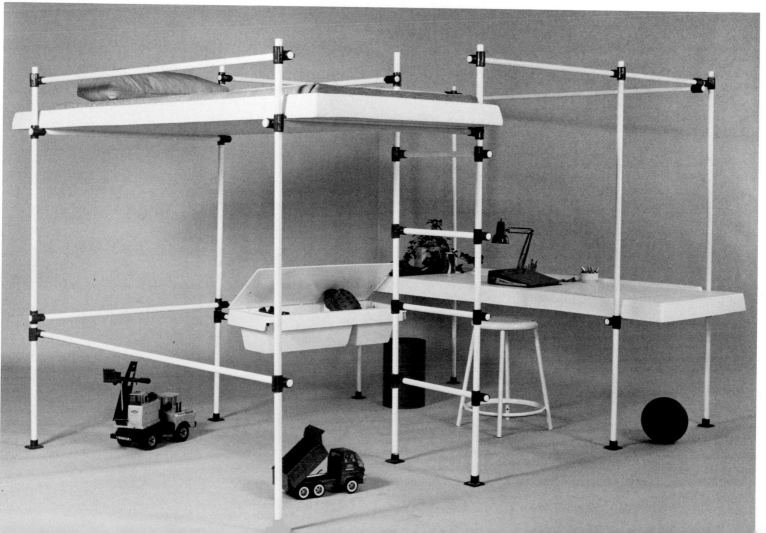

This room for Robert has a clear-lacquered birch elevated bed over shelving and a desk of the same material. The adjacent platforms and floor are covered with gray Tretford carpeting. Design is by Noel Jeffrey.

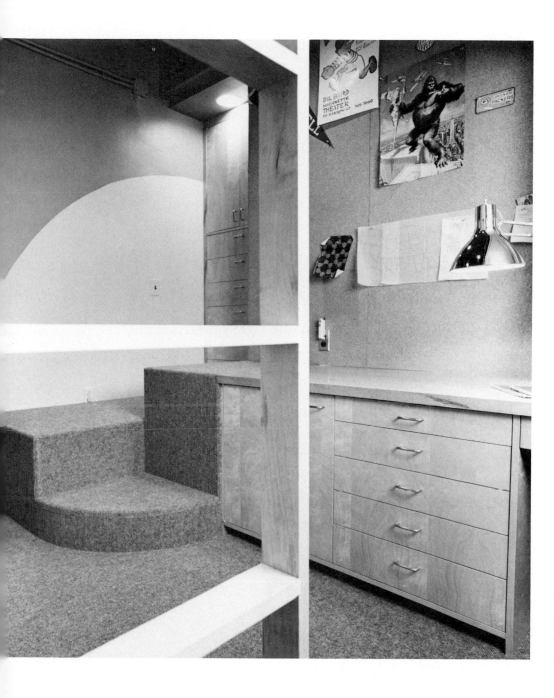

The longer, carpeted platform opens up for storage and, with a sleeping bag, doubles as a cozy niche for an overnight guest. Originally the space was a small maid's room in this New York apartment.

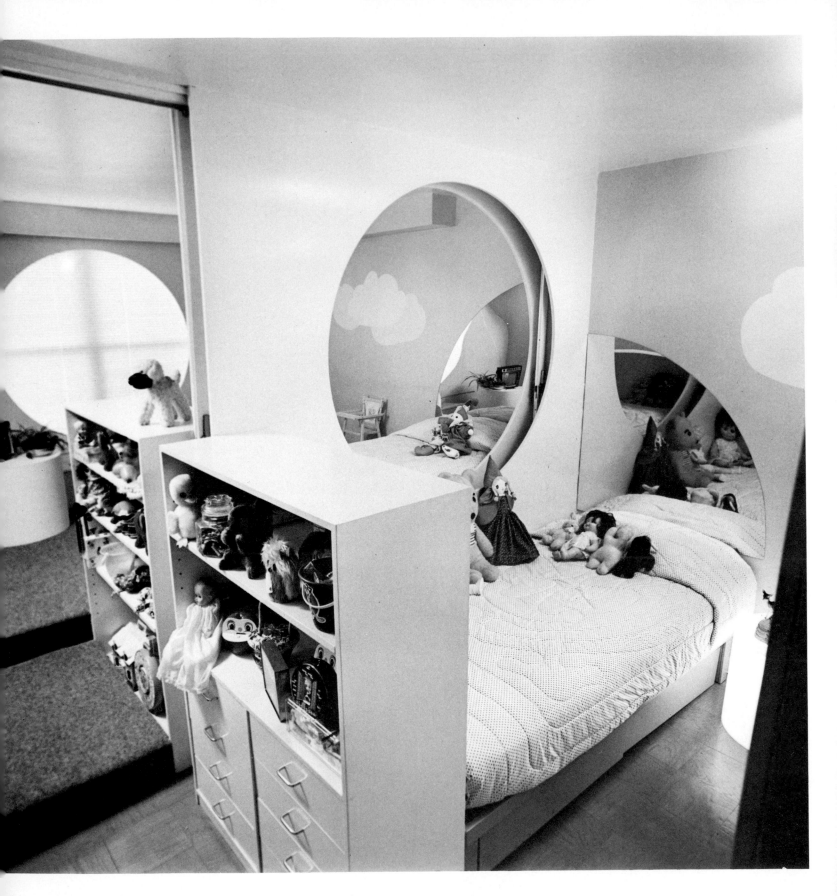

In the room he designed for Lauren, Noel Jeffrey shows how a small bedroom can be successfully shared by a child and an adult. The room is predominantly pink with painted clouds on the wall and polka-dot bedspreads to complete the effect of softness in shapes and surfaces. Quarter-circles of mirror next to the beds make the room seem larger than it is. Sliding plywood panels separate the two spaces when necessary. During the day, when the circle is open, Lauren and her friends can jump through from bed to bed.

Rosemary Songer

A room in a typical New York apartment can seem anonymous and constricting unless you find a way to make the most of one or two features. This children's room is in a third-floor apartment and has two nice windows and a rather high ceiling. The platform reduces the windowsill height, creating a cozy seating area and making possible a more direct view to the sidewalk trees below.

The requirements for the design of this little girls' room were presented to me mainly by their mother, who felt that each one should have her own separate study area and place to put her favorite things. She also requested a shared work area that didn't have to be cleaned up every day. The third specification was for a space where visiting children could sleep. That's one reason that we carpeted the level next to the lower bed.

The girls seem happy with the ways I satisfied those requests, but what pleases me more is that they have found new ways of using the room—ways that never occurred to me. I believe that if a space is well designed that should happen—that its true usefulness is continually being discovered by the people who live and work there, far beyond what the designer planned.

In Jennifer and Karen's room designed by Rosemary Songer, the three desks, one of which is seen in the mirror here, give added privacy and permit unfinished projects to remain undisturbed while both girls do their homework. The mirror, center, is framed by two blue bulletin boards made of Homosote. (See also page 130.)

This room, designed by Joan Regenbogen, makes extensive use of gray shag carpeting, giving it an appealing look and providing good sound absorption for the activities of her musician son. White Formica desk top and cabinets complete the room.

At some point, most teen-agers decide they want their rooms to look more like sitting rooms than bedrooms. This pink-and-green room by Noel Jeffrey shows all the signs of transition that such rooms usually represent. The familiar stuffed animals still nestle in a corner of the sofa bed, yet the orderly arrangement of belongings, the telephone, and the fresh flowers on the small table suggest that Betsy is more adult now than child.

Owen Beenhouwer designs rooms that are as
streamlined for teen-agers as his nursery
rooms are whimsical and amusing for
younger children. In this one, painted yellow
and orange (opposite), the circular
openings cut out of plywood provide easy
access to display spaces and frame the
entrance to the room. Two beds tucked neatly
into corners of the room leave ample floor
space for spreading out games and projects.
Suspended globe lights attach to a U-shaped
ceiling track.

146

Owen Beenhouwer transformed a large dark
room into a cheerful, well-lit one enlivened by
bright colors. To lend a greater sense of
space, he placed all elements along the
perimeter of the room and kept them light and
open in appearance. Two ladders lead to the
level above the closets where the top bunk is.
From there, one can slide down to the
bed below.

The mirror in Maggie's room reflects light pouring into the room through vertical blinds on windows facing east, behind the camera. She is delighted with the feeling of openness and light created in her room by Martin Rich, and with the stepped storage system and neat vanity table.

A full, room-width desk in front of the window completes the furnishings along with a studio bed. The ceiling is lowered except for a central panel seen at the left. In addition, she has a giant walk-in closet for clothes and miscellaneous sports equipment. Cabinetry by Steve Milom.

Robert A. M. Stern

The worst thing is to try to second-guess children. They usually know what they like, though they are not always able to say what they want. I believe in designing rooms so that people—children and adults alike—can add to them over time. I want to give them opportunities to use the objects they love and collect. You shouldn't overprogram a room, especially a child's room: Children keep growing and changing, which is as it should be.

The room that my nine-year-old son has now was designed just before he was born. It still works very well—because it isn't cute and kiddielike. It's simple, with lots of open shelves and storage space. His play table has just been replaced with a desk. Apart from this, no changes have been made; the room is as useful now as it ever was.

A small child's room should be a place where a child can play creatively on his own—probably on the floor. My experience as a child and my son's have been the same: Never play at a table when you can play on the floor. My son's room is always filled with constructions and toys. He uses toys in ways never imagined by the manufacturers. He takes them apart and makes new toys.

Sometimes, however, circumstances force one to abandon theory. A few years ago, when a client's son was about nine, *he* wanted an all-black room. When he told me this, I turned to his parents and asked, "What should I do?" They replied, "He's the client." So I thought fast and said, "What's your second favorite color?" "Red" was the answer.

After a moment of panic, I went to work. The red room turned out to be quite original and specifically related to the inhabitant's needs at the time. Perhaps too much so.

Eventually the old red room and the sleeping bags on platforms no longer appealed. We're working on a new scheme now for the room that will be better suited to the occupant's more grown-up needs. In its specificity, the red room was an exception to my rule. Nonetheless, the red room was a success in the sense that it represented an ambience in which that child could live comfortably—an ambience not so restricted that an unmade bed or one more poster of the Fonz could wreak havoc and compromise the "integrity" of the room, nor so loose that it offered the occupant no clues about how the room might be used. It tells us about the boy who lived there, about the things that interested him then, about the kind of kid he is—and it tells a bit about the architect who designed it as well. But then, if people grow and change, I suppose rooms and architects must also. . . .

So I've talked myself around full circle, haven't I?

At night, instead of a bed, Robert A. M. Stern's young client snuggles into a sleeping bag spread out on the mattress platforms shown in center foreground. The sleeping bag and the boy's clothes are kept in drawers on the desk side of the partition. Vertical hanging space is available in the closet near the door to the room. In accordance with the boy's wishes, all surfaces and fabrics in this room, including the carpeting, are bright red. Four adjustable Luxo lamps provide infinite lighting variations.

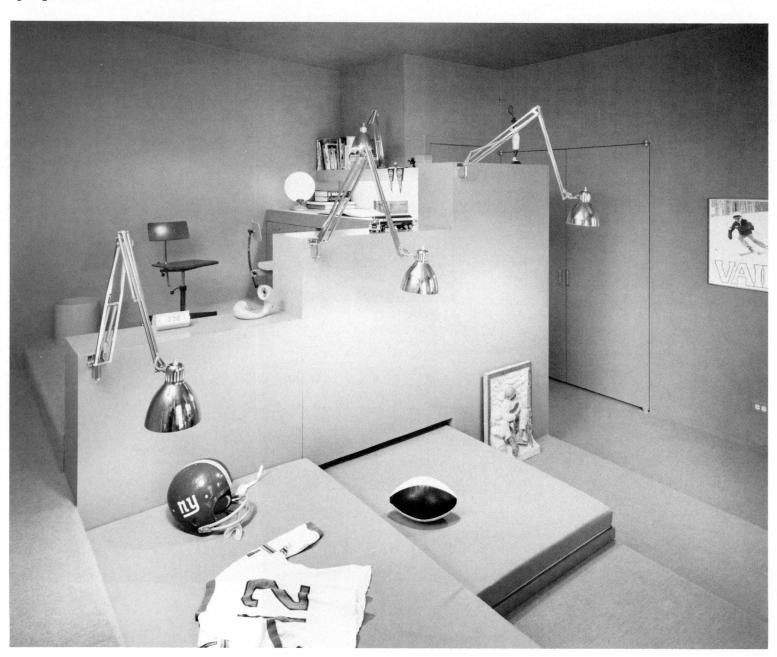

This monochromatic room by Robert Stern can sleep three full-size teen-agers. The canopylike bunk above the bed is reached by climbing the ladder built into the side of the storage unit. A trundle bed pulls out when required from below the ''middle'' bed. Small stereo speakers sit neatly on the shelf above the bed. The space is entirely blue and white. *(Photograph by E. Stoecklein)*

In this room for a little girl, Robert Stern combines the traditional pink-and-white-for-girls color scheme with a totally modern, architectural approach to the space. The white stripes along the walls are actually Homosote strips—ideal for bulletin boards. The pocket door leads from the elevated desk area to the adjacent bathroom, conveniently located for cleaning up messy art projects. White Formica is used for the built-in cabinetry. The upper level and steps are white-painted tongue-and-groove flooring. *(Photograph by E. Stoecklein)*

Robert Harper
for Moore Grover Harper

A man's house is his castle and a child's room is his or her castle. The room is a house in miniature and should fill many of the same needs of the child as the house fills for the adult.

One of those needs is personal habitation—the making of a place of one's own, but with the further complication that the child's manner of habitation will change from year to year. Think of a child's room as a shell or stage to be inhabited by the child over a period of years. As the child grows older the roles he plays will change, and the furnishings which are the sets will change, too. If we have done our jobs properly, the room will not only be a stimulating visual and spatial environment, but also a place where this change in habitation can occur.

We have usually been constrained (happily, it often turns out) by low budgets into keeping rooms simple rather than complex—into designing with light and space rather than with elegant materials. This makes changes easier in the long run.

Another need is for privacy, often at several levels. To the child, the living room may be Main Street and the playroom (if there is one) the first level of space over which he has some control. In his own room his control of the environment expands. We have often gone upstairs to what might have been attic space to gain a second layer of privacy. The downstairs area can be kept more or less presentable for the parents and the upstairs space (particularly if it is difficult for grown-ups to get to) is quite private and the child's own.

Finally, I think it's worth suggesting that our best children's rooms are done when we ourselves are most open to the needs for change, for privacy, and for the particular furnishings for children. We are perhaps least successful when pursuing our own concerns to the exclusion of the children's. We have tried, in our designs for houses, to encourage children to share their visions of places with us so that their rooms can become more their designs than ours.

These two rooms, each with their own interconnecting upper levels, were designed by Moore Grover Harper. The spaces are identical but one is the reverse of the other. The very compact lower level includes a large walk-in closet as well as the bed and desk unit. The carpeting behind the ladder is there to prevent scuff marks on the wall. The upper level is primarily for recreation in this Connecticut house.

This irregularly shaped room with its stepped platform bed below a giant poster was designed by MLTW/Moore-Turnbull for a teen-aged boy. The space has a skylight above the bed and a second large window (not shown) overlooking the upper part of the living room. The multicolored storage units extend to the right, ultimately becoming a desk.

A fabric from Jack Lenor Larsen, Inc., covers the walls of Ellen's New York City bedroom. The leaf pattern extends to the window curtains and appears again, in reverse colors, on Ellen's bedspread. Even the fragment of carpet near the bed picks up the leaf motif. In this room, designer Alan Buchsbaum satisfied his client's request for a four-poster bed in a contemporary setting.

160

The upper level to the room by MLTW/
Moore-Turnbull was added after the house
had been completed and is just large enough
for a double bed. From this sleeping balcony
one has a beautiful view of the Long Island
Sound. Oddly shaped shutters control the
sunlight coming into the room. The
supergraphic is by Mary Ann Rumney.

Adult guests feel quite at home in this room by MLTW/Moore-Turnbull while the occupant is off at college. The room has its own bathroom behind the stair and is in the same Connecticut house as the one on page 157.

Another irregularly shaped space, this one by Charles Moore and Richard Oliver, is in the same New Jersey house as the rooms shown on pages 32 and 45. The beautifully painted floor, complete with waterfall, is by David Cohn, New York City.

Architect Carl Weinbroer shares his office
with his son, Kirtley, age three. During the
day, Weinbroer uses the desk, storage space,
and reference books in this small rectangular
room. Kirtley enjoys playing at his father's
feet while his mother is away teaching. In the
evening, the fabric elephant is folded up, the
panel on the right pulls down revealing a
bed, and Kirtley has the room to himself for
the night.

In city apartments, the spaciousness of the old-fashioned nursery is hard to find. Beds are the principal thieves of space. It occurred to architects Howard Korenstein and Alan Buchsbaum that if the beds could be eliminated, except at night, their client would have all the space she could possibly need for games and activities. Their solution was to use Murphy beds concealed behind folding doors in the daytime. Commercial-style door pulls from Elmer T. Hebert, New York City, are used on the doors.

At night the doors in Winifred's room are easily opened and not one but two full-size beds appear with covers of Marimekko fabric to match the window shades. Strips of birch board over the bed are useful for displaying favorite items of art. More birch-board strips frame panels of wallpaper, designed by Alan Buchsbaum for Norton Blumenthal, forming a border around Winifred's room and her brother's.

Though Winifred and her brother, Carter, have separate rooms, the two spaces can be joined for special events such as miniature stock-car races. The decorative motifs are the same in both rooms. Carter's bed sits firmly on the floor so he can easily grab a quick daytime nap, and a trundle bed fits neatly underneath it. Yellow Tretford carpeting is used in both rooms. On the right, a painted blackboard is set behind the sliding door.

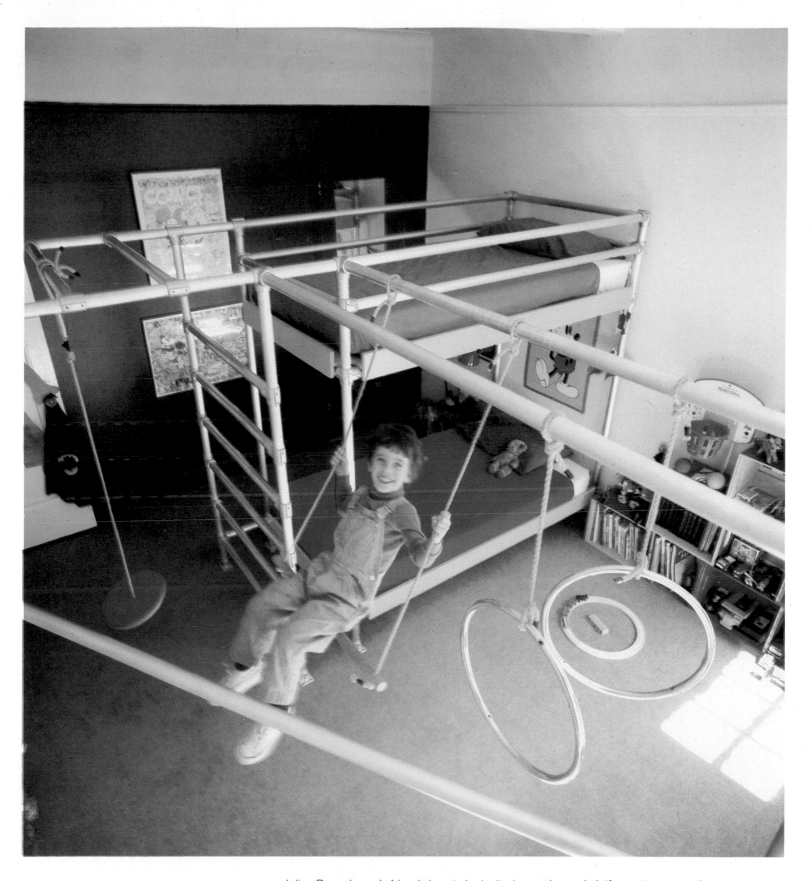

Julian Boxenbaum's friends love to be invited to play on the jungle gym designed for him by his father, architect Charles Boxenbaum. To build the gym frame, Boxenbaum used 1½-inch diameter aluminum pipe with Speed-Rail connectors from the A. E. Hollaender Company in Cincinnati, Ohio. He added plywood platforms to support the two mattresses, aluminum rings found in the street, a homemade trapeze, and a swing made from a barrel top. The pipes need to be cleaned once to remove the shop coating and the brand name. After that, the unit is virtually maintenance free.

A four-section mobile storage wall can solve many problems. This one, designed by Stephan Marc Klein, neatly defines a child's play area at one end of the parents' large living room. On one side it is a display cabinet for a photographer's antique camera collection as well as a surface for mounting art objects. On the other side it has shelves for his two children's toys with a desk for sit-down projects such as puzzle-solving (see opposite). The unit can also be fully extended to make a folding partition.

The other, living-room side of this folding storage wall presents a smooth facade for displaying art, with small triangular shelves that are also corner braces to position the hinged segments. (See opposite.) On this side, it forms a play space for Sophie and Sebastien. Made of hollow-core doors, the segments have holes drilled along the edges at distances of one inch, allowing placement of more triangular shelves as desired on the children's side. The outer hinged sections can be folded inward to form a four-sided enclosed box.

171

A Formica-surfaced slide, a rope ladder from
Creative Playthings, and plywood panels
painted dark blue with circles cut out of them
fit into the basic jungle-gym frame designed
by Charles Boxenbaum to complete Timmy's
indoor playground. Other variations are
possible, depending on where the joints of
the pipe are located. "A feature of the Speed-
Rail joints," says architect Boxenbaum, "is
their closed ends. This makes the joints safe
to handle, substantially reducing the risk of
injury to children playing on them." The
supergraphic flag was painted on the wall by
Timmy's parents.

Henry Smith - Miller

In designing for children, I try to remember my own favorite spaces as a child. I think of the afternoons I spent reorganizing my parents' furniture into castles or tents with the help of an occasional blanket. In this world of my own making, I first learned about scale and space and became aware of myself as an individual with changing needs and desires.

The program requirements for the Box involved storage space, three beds (two for occasional guests), a study/work area, space for plants, an aquarium, and finally a private space for the child alone. The child was eighteen months old when we began to design the Box, and his parents stipulated a life expectancy of ten years for the Box, so the changing size of the client, the child, became a significant design factor.

We proposed a room within a playroom, a castle with windows, a ladder, two levels, a bridge, cubbyholes, and a fold-down desk (an intellectual drawbridge) to be closed down during sleeping hours. The box was scaled to the size of the child, yet all parts of it are accessible to adults for cleaning.

The Box sits in the middle of the playroom on a painted floor. One entire wall of the playroom is covered in Formica for diagrams and drawings; the other has a mirror which reflects the round window. The floor within the box has a soft carpeted surface. The Box itself is made of natural-finish birch plywood.

As the Box was to be installed in the shortest time possible and could not be built on site, a system of prefabricated panels small enough to fit in the elevator was decided upon. The cabinetmaker assembled the entire structure in our architectural studio for a preinstallation check, and then delivered and installed the Box in two days.

The Box is essentially a giant toy to be lived in and on, and played with. It is a castle, a jungle gym, a library, a living room. It is something that can become for the child almost anything he dreams of. Yet this total physical and imaginative environment was not very expensive to create.

A trundle bed beneath Jeremy's bed brings the number of sleeping spaces in the Box to three—there is another bed on top of the cube. Though the cube can be taken apart, assembled it is sturdy enough for climbing and other acrobatics. (See also page 188.)

The cantilevered table pivots upward to enclose the shelving above. The underside becomes a cork bulletin board when the table is closed. The panel along the top of the cube is white Formica. The chairs, designed by Alvar Aalto, are available from International Contract Furnishings, Inc.

Another variation on the bed-storage system is this freestanding unit by Owen Beenhouwer for his son. Here, David sleeps in princely splendor above the open storage shelves and the low closet on the far side of his bed. The sturdy rungs and rails are from a marine-supply store. A rope ladder to a level built over the door offers still more opportunities for climbing and exploring. Cork tile is used on the floor of this New York brownstone.

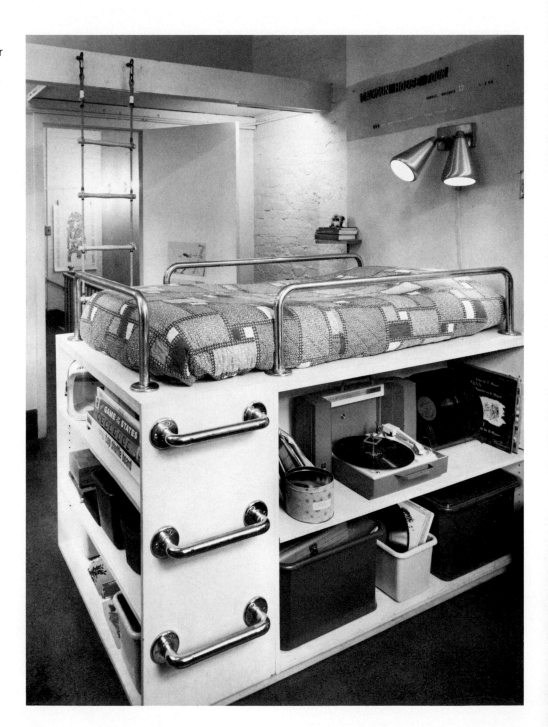

Originally Myron and June Goldfinger, parents of Thira and Djerba, slept in this giant, yellow four-poster bed. When the little girls outgrew the cribs of their infancy, it seemed an appealing idea for them to share the huge bed rather than have separate sleeping quarters at a stage when they enjoyed being together. So Myron and June moved upstairs to a new bedroom above the treetops, and the girls took over the four-poster. Each girl has her own desk and additional storage space in built-in units not shown in this view.

Penny and Jim Hull believe that furniture for
children should have many uses. Beds, for
example, should be for studying and drawing,
reading, lolling around—not just for sleeping.
This sofa bed designed by the Hulls is tailor-
made for teen-agers who enjoy its enveloping
design and informal feeling. It consists of a
simple, open U-shaped, tubular steel frame
with canvas stretched over it, supporting a
mattress and coordinated throw pillows.
Available from the H.U.D.D.L.E. stores
in California.

Designed by Henry Smith-Miller and Michael
Rubin, this approximately eight-foot-square
cube known as the Box is built of birch-
veneer plywood with a hand-rubbed
polyurethane finish. The movable ladder leads
to a bed on the cube's top level. The Box has
its own electrical system. It can be taken apart
easily and reassembled in another space. The
strip-oak floor is painted with blue deck paint.
(See also pages 181-183.)

Paul Laird

It grows up from three points and sprouts barrels. Tricornered, rounded, over-whelming, and yet comical. But what is it for? Who cares, as long as it amuses people, and it does.

Take an end view: There is a man standing with his big feet turned out in the Chaplinesque manner, wearing high-waisted pants with a double row of buttons just under the armpits. He has enormous floppy ears.

Children embrace this thing, measure its curves with their whole bodies, experience precarious adventures, find comfort, lie across the top barrels as though riding a mother whale, slide down into the hammock in the middle out of view, drop through a hole into the teahouse, squeeze in between the barrels, climb in the storage bins, and sit there like peas in a pod.

Did I say teahouse? Oh, yes. That's where the downstairs is. When you duck under the barrels you find yourself in a place of shelter and arresting simplicity, suitable for six of us and I don't know how many of them!

My friend Michael Melitonov is the builder. I am the designer. We constructed the piece without drawings for a client who wanted a structure for his children to play on. Some ideas had to be abandoned or reshaped as we went along. It was a case of finding what the materials could do, as neither of us had ever bent a piece of plywood before. The first models had to be scrapped. So did the budget. When we were well in over our heads, Melitonov would muse, "Oh, come now, Mr. X, wouldn't you really rather have a Buick?"

We persevered. The client threatened suit. I managed to raise enough money to redeem his losses and become the owner of the Vehicular Bedroom.

It served, for a while, as a place for my daughter, Rachel, to sleep when she came to visit in my 50-by-100-foot loft. It had the advantage of being movable, so we could push it to one side to make space for a game of tennis or badminton.

Now that Rachel no longer uses it, the V.H. has no particular function other than being decorative and amusing. I consider it a public piece now.

At first glance, this massive 250-pound construction appears to be a rolling sculpture, or jungle gym. It is these things and many more, but it once served as a sleeping space for its creator's daughter, Rachel.

Designed by Paul Laird, it was constructed with the help of Michael Melitonov, a sculptor and builder. During a period when Rachel visited her father on weekends, she used the lower level of the unit as a sleep deck with a macramé hanging just barely visible in the photograph as a hammock-canopy. Bedding and Rachel's belongings were kept in the six horizontal barrels that hinge open for convenient storage.

The vehicular bedroom is made of marine-grade mahogany plywood painted gray; it has wheels and can easily be moved, even by a child.

The bed-storage unit designed by
Christopher Owen for his daughter Tjasa has
beds on two levels. Shelves at the foot of one
bed accommodate Tjasa's growing library.
Her dollhouse is prominently displayed on a
special platform in the foreground of the
photograph. Open shelves at the head of the
bed are perfect for displaying treasures,
particularly Tjasa's collection of miniature
animals. The curtain with colored outlines of
animals and a broad stripe of yellow across
the ceiling and down one wall complement
the neutral tones of the bed and storage units
as well as the white walls and floor.

In Switzerland we had seen dollhouses mounted on the wall and displayed as shadow boxes. We had wanted a dollhouse for our daughter, May, for a long time, but had little floor space to accommodate it. Putting it on the wall, in the kitchen where May and her brother most often play, seemed like a lovely idea. My husband, Kent, designed it so that we could open and close the window behind it.

—NONA BLOOMER

Our daughter, May's, dollhouse has both a private and a public quality in relation to our house and the rest of the family. Essentially, the dollhouse is a private territory governed by May. It is a part of our house that she has control over and can express herself in. But it is part of our house; it is not sequestered away in May's room where no one but she can enjoy it. Putting the dollhouse where we did, in a passageway that we all use, gave it a public quality, like a house on a street. In the morning all of us can see the sun shining through the windows of May's domain, just as we can see it shining from the same direction through the rest of the house. The presence of this miniature house in a public place allows us to view the world outside through the collections of our daughter's imagination.

—KENT BLOOMER

OUTDOOR ENVIRONMENTS

When children play together, creating environments for themselves is as much a part of what they do as making up games, songs, and rituals. Young children will play house in any space they consider suitable. They might mark off rooms with blocks, or stones under a tree, or even rows of piled-up fallen leaves.

As children grow older, the environments become more sophisticated. The houses that take shape at the hands of these young architects are not usually copies of the houses they actually live in. They reflect lively imaginations that have not yet been harnessed with consideration for too many "trivial" practical matters.

Biologists recognize that the need to make a place for ourselves is a basic form of adaptive behavior. It comes very early in life and is expressed first with building blocks and "indoor" toys, then, frequently out-of-doors, with whatever materials the child can lay his hands on. In the country children use pieces of wood, old boxes and tires, bits of rope to make private places for themselves. City children, too, use whatever discards they can commandeer for their building projects. T. H. Sorenson, a landscape architect in Denmark, noticed, more than twenty-five years ago, that children were frequently more intrigued by the building materials left at the sites of playgrounds than by the playgrounds themselves. Sorenson felt that children should be allowed to be their own builders. The "adventure playground" he designed, based on this concept, is still in existence outside of Copenhagen and has served as a model for similar playgrounds in England, Western Europe, and the United States.

In 1976, Nancy Renfro received a grant from the National Endowment for the Arts to encourage children to learn about architecture. She went into classrooms of children aged seven to twelve and devised projects for them. One of her assignments for them was to draw a hideaway for two, anywhere in the world. The only special requirements were that it had to have a secret entrance without a key, and it had to be decorated inside.

Two results of this assignment are shown. The one with the artificial sun, page 196, is by Stephanie Broomhall and Renee Bakeslee. The underwater hideaway is by Kelli Kenny and Meg Boericke. Both drawings show the boundless imagination of children at this age. They suggest what children's priorities might be in their environment—if anything were possible.

Don Wall is an architect and teacher who believes that the building instinct of children is potentially a basis for all forms of early learning. Like Jean Piaget, the Swiss educator—who said that in a multisensory situation the intellect grows, the mind is able to grasp disciplines of thought and proceed to higher levels of understanding—Wall maintains that children learn about themselves and about life by physically putting things together. He sees a close relationship between the concepts of building things and those of learning to read and do arithmetic. Wall has set up early-learning architectual programs for preschoolers in Maryland and New Jersey. The children he works with make their own "buildings" from the materials he provides, sometimes in less than two hours.

And then there are tree houses—perhaps the closest most children come to making a house for themselves, a real building with four walls and a roof, a place where one feels separate from the world and yet, literally and figuratively, *above* it. The tree house may be the ultimate child's environment, designed and built by himself, for himself and the chosen few with whom he is willing to share it. A tree house or similarly complete outdoor structure in the family garden or backyard is often a sign that the child, while not rejecting his indoor environment, is ready to move beyond it to make his own place and to lead his own life.

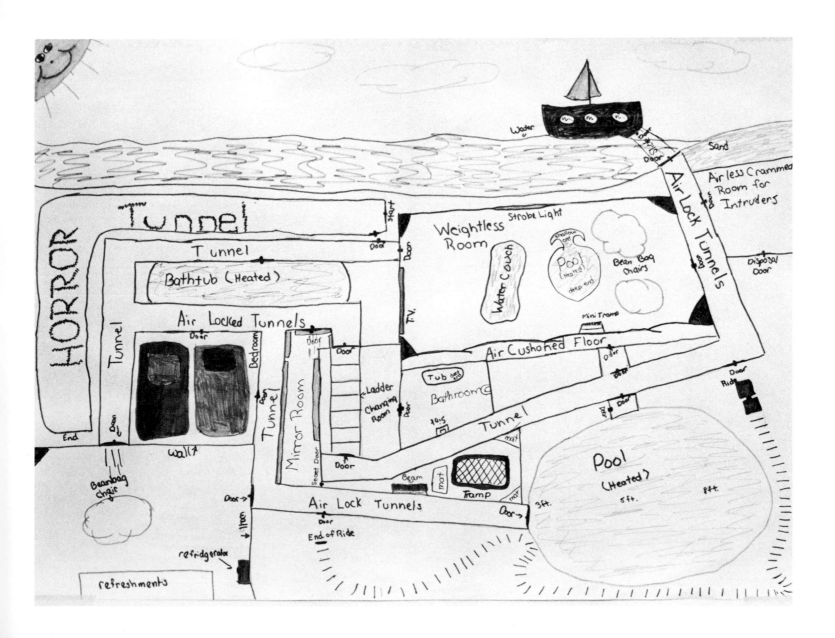

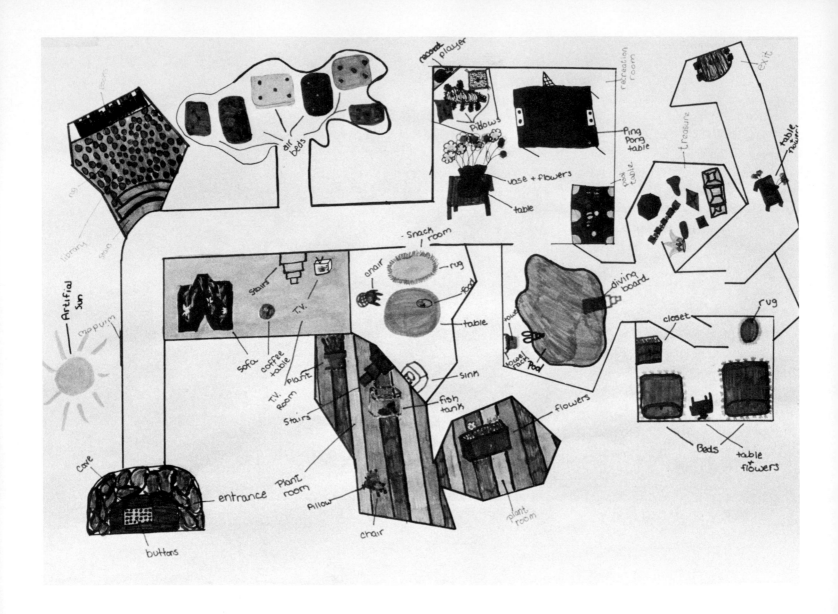

rug
record player
recreation room
exit
library
Pillows
Ping Pong table
treasure
table tower
air beds
pool table
vase + flowers
table
Snack room
chair
rug
food
diving board
Artifial Sun
mopuim
stairs
T.V.
table
towel rack
Pool
rug
closet
sofa
coffee table
plant
sink
fish tank
flowers
T.V. room
Stairs
Plant room
Pillow
chair
plant room
Beds
table + flowers
cave
entrance
buttons

Opposite: Adventure Playground, Irvine, California.

"Perhaps more than anything else, youngsters need to make an impact on their environment: to get the feel of it, to mold it, to make it change before their eyes, and to master it. They constantly invent and improvise, dismantling things and wrecking them or putting things together and making them work."

Jeanette Galambos Stone and Nancy Rudolph in *Play and Playgrounds*, National Association for the Education of Young Children, 1970.

An outdoor environment can be an elevated box mounted on the stump of an oak tree killed by gypsy moths. Ian Harper helped his father, Robert Harper, build this one within swinging distance of a wood climbing frame. The box is open at the top, lending itself to use as a watchtower when Ian and his friends are playing on the hillside.

Don Wall

Everyone should be able to express themselves in their own environment, especially children. Jean Piaget, the Swiss educator, has pointed out that children conceive of the world in quite different terms from adults. Why should they spend so many years of their lives living in spaces scaled for much bigger people, surrounded by objects that scarcely relate to their size at all?

Children, spontaneously, like to build. Building things provides a focus for all the child's developing skills: A child who is old enough to walk and talk can grasp things, place them, make them fit. The experience of building gives children the opportunity to use all these skills to make a world equal in their minds to their parents' world. The world that children build for themselves is one that they feel comfortable in. The process of building it helps children to understand not only how things work in that world, but also in the larger one that they share with their parents.

Building in a classroom situation does more than offer children insights into their own environment. It gets them involved in extended thinking. Children learn to visualize something that does not yet exist. They plan it, organize it, define the problems of making it, and resolve them. They become highly motivated to acquire each skill necessary to bring the project to reality. A child who sets out to build something that is 30 feet long with a room to sleep in at one end and a fort at the other—a stretched-out space over which he has control—learns something about orientation in space and time. He develops spatial memory, relating one space that is far away to the one he is standing in at that moment. Gradually, he becomes able to retain such information over longer and larger thought and time spaces. It seems to me that this ability can be usefully applied to learning to read, to doing arithmetic, studying geography, history, and eventually any kind of information.

Working together on a building project, children also learn the meaning of adaptability and flexibility. They come to understand concepts of group behavior, sharing, and team effort that they might not otherwise grasp until they were much older. The opportunities for positive intellectual and social experiences are endless, but the important thing is really not precisely what the children are learning; it is the fact that they are learning by *doing*, by trial and error in many cases, by physically using the materials available to them in a variety of self-determined, constructive ways.

Jean Piaget decided, in the course of two large volumes of study, that spatial cognition is the basis of all knowledge. If this is so, can there be any doubt about the value of developing a sense of one's self in relation to spaces at the earliest possible age? Why should nearly-adult architecture and design students be the only people to have the opportunity to explore concepts that are at once so fascinating and so useful? By connecting with the child's early impulse to build, and sustaining this connection, we will be educating children to be more resourceful, sensitive, and creative. And we'll probably have better buildings someday, too.

Any born tree climber can get to this tree house in Austin, Texas, but ladies are requested to remove high heels. Designed for painters Owen and Judy Cappelman, this tree house was quickly claimed by their children, though there is yet another one for them, higher up, in the live oak. Design, decoration, construction, and photography by architect Richard Oliver.

"Children love to build," says Don Wall, "and child-conceived and child-built architecture differs radically from what adults give them." Wall introduces nursery-school children to basic concepts of architecture with a building board that has holes in it. He gives them flowers in tubes that fit into the holes. Then the children are invited to arrange the flowers on the board in any way they like.

Wall points out to the children that if the sun gets too hot, the flowers will wilt. If there is a storm, they may blow away. The flowers must be protected. The children are provided with poles and sheets to make walls and a roof.

At last, a shelter for the flowers is made. Its form is determined by its function. The flowers are safe under the sloping white roof the children designed for them, with no more sun than they need. *(Photographs by Don Wall)*

As walls and a roof protect flowers, so they shelter children, too. The hardworking young architects enjoy their lunch in the shady comfort of their own open-air dining room. *(Photograph by Don Wall)*

Lady Allen of Hurtwood

The movement for adventure playgrounds in England arose as a constructive protest against the sterile playgrounds of asphalt and mechanical equipment to which most of our city children are condemned and which so many adults consider adequate for boisterous, adventurous children. Adventure playgrounds were also started as a way to use the country's many bomb sites for play, rather than for parking lots or merely as derelict eyesores for the free dumping of rubbish.

Nearly all the adventure playgrounds were started and are run by autonomous groups of parents and other helpers, drawn mostly from the immediate neighborhood. The majority are on wasteland waiting development and are, therefore, held on short leases of five to ten years.

The essence of an adventure playground is that it is an area where children and young people can do most of the things they want to do, for which they have a deep, perhaps unconscious urge. That is, all children, the world over, have a passion to build houses and dens where they can live their own private lives. For this they must have an ample supply of timber, nails, hammers, and saws, and even potentially dangerous tools like pickaxes and chisels. They want to dig deep holes, down to Australia perhaps, to tunnel through the earth and to make caves to creep into. . . . The joy of an adventure playground is that there is no end to the things that can be attempted. Some projects are started and never completed, and some go out of fashion, but there is life and excitement, and change all the time. Nothing is static and nothing is man-made; all is improvised.

In summary, all the adventure playgrounds have grown up independently and all differ significantly. All, however, aim to absorb the interest and release the energies of young people and are based on a common theme of enabling children to handle malleable materials in their own way, in a free and permissive atmosphere. They work with real tools and take calculated risks without fear of criticisim or censure.

From "Adventure Playgrounds" by Lady Allen of Hurtwood,
an essay in *Small Urban Spaces*, edited by W. N. Seymour, Jr.,
New York University Press, New York, 1969.

In building their houses, forts, clubhouses, children sometimes show the same values their parents do in choosing or building their houses. These children in an adventure playground in Irvine, California, took care to put their house at a respectable distance from the noisy skateboard run just over the fence. Though the small house in the photograph has a prominent "picture window," the rest of it is becoming well enclosed, showing the builders' interest in privacy. The walls seem to signify a desire to be separate from the neighbors ("KEEP OUT"), yet this structure is one of several that grow up in clusters around the playground (page 197), suggesting that, even at an early age, children want to be part of a community.

Even a city child can have a playhouse in the backyard if he has a grandfather as clever as Gabriella and Christopher's. Max Mandell built this playhouse with split-rail fencing, four metal posts sunk in concrete, and a few wood crossbeams. He used redwood slatting inside the playhouse, and green corrugated fiber glass for the roof. Indoor-outdoor carpeting, available at most large department stores, and some standard playground equipment complete this small-scale outdoor environment. Gabriella and Christopher played there often as young children. Now that they are teen-agers, the little playground is used by their mother for her nursery-school class.

Is it a rocket ship ready for takeoff? No, it's a tool shed. Impossible? Not really, it's a playhouse, too. Designed by Hugh Hardy, it stands in the woods behind the Hardys' house in Massachusetts. At least two children can sleep there on a hot summer night, or climb and hide in its nooks and crannies during the day. The ramp by the door is there for a reason. This is a bicycle shed, too.

Penelope and her friend, Helen, look down on
the intruder from an apparently unreachable
height inside the Hardy three-story tower.
This is a place where children can play alone
for hours, unsupervised and undisturbed.

No matter how perfect their indoor environment, children need a place to retreat to from the rest of the world. With this in mind, David Robinson and his son designed and built this two-story trellised tower. The tower makes a sculpturelike addition to the Robinsons' California garden of fruit trees and evergreens.

The fact that a child picks a tree to build in, rather than building on the ground, suggests that the tree means something special to him. The appeal of the tree lies in the fact that it keeps growing and moving. Each generation of kids gets into the tree house and remodels it. Often, the older kids will hand it down to the younger ones with secret rituals.
—DAVID STILES *(author of* Huts and Hideaways*)*
in "Tree Houses Just for Fun" by Georgia Dullea,
The New York Times, *April 14, 1977. Copyright ©*
by The New York Times.

As David Stiles became increasingly involved in building a tree house for his children, he wondered why more grown-ups don't build them for themselves. How else could one achieve this sense of seclusion, but also of dominance, that being in a tree house offers?

So the Stiles tree house became a family place, complete with sauna and modest facilities for eating and sleeping. Whoever said that tree houses were for children only? *(Photograph by Eddy Sun)*

213

"It's anything and everything I think is best
Because, when I climb to my house in the tree
I pretend it's whatever I want it to be."

From The Wonderful Tree House *by Harold Longman.*
Text Copyright © 1962. By permission of Parents'
Magazine Press.

214

Even though Amy Carter has a lovely bed in the White House, she occasionally slips out on a hot summer night to sleep in her tree house. Designed by her father, Jimmy, who is also President of the United States, Amy's hideaway is actually a freestanding platform on four sturdy posts, not supported by the branches of the 40-foot cedar that shades it. Amy climbs along the outstretched lower limbs to reach her hidden perch above, complete with hammock, to view the Washington Monument and the city beyond.

Nicky Koenig
(age sixteen)

There's something about a tree house that makes it different from any other kind of structure. A tree house appeals to everyone's sense of fantasy and imagination. It isn't difficult to build a tree house, and because it is raised from the ground, there are all kinds of design possibilities that don't exist with a normal building.

After building the tree house, I went on to attempt a real house simply because I needed a place to stay for a long period of time here on the farm. My friend and I didn't really know how to begin; we had no specific plan for the interior, we just put windows and doors wherever we felt they belonged.

Now my friend has gone off to build bigger and better things and I am left to deal with the product of one summer's excited but naïve architectural efforts. It falls to me to make oddly shaped windows and doors conform with one another and to learn some useful lessons by trying to correct the errors resulting from our lack of planning.

I still dream of building a house that is a unity of softly flowing angles and dimensions, depth and height, light and shadow. Because I have this dream, I continue to build.

"To be in a tree house is to be inside and yet outside, to be free and yet protected, to be up in the air and yet rooted, held. It is a distant retreat, yet conveniently near. It is being adventurous and yet homeloving, a wayfarer and nest builder, a pirate and a lighthouse keeper. Tree houses enclose all the spirit which needs enclosure and liberate all the spirit that needs to see horizon from horizon and guess what lies beyond."

From Tree Houses: An Illustrated Essay on the Aesthetic and Practical Aspects of Arboreal Architecture, *The Green Tiger Press, La Jolla, California,* © *1975.*

Nicky Koenig's California tree house was built with an older friend when Nicky was thirteen years old. Using apple boxes from the surrounding orchards and redwood shingles, the structure is lashed to the living tree without a single nail. Three years and many wild storms later, the tree house is still intact though the tree is somewhat the worse for wear.

217

This view of the inside of Nicky Koenig's tree house shows the lashed framework and the painstaking weatherproofing with tar paper. The tree trunk and straw mat are now the only furnishings. The window affords a beautiful mountaintop view of apple orchards and redwoods.

Spurred on by the success of his building efforts in his tree house, and supported by adults who recognize his talent, sixteen-year-old Nick Koenig is now building his own house. It is the product of thoughtful planning, detailed and accurate perspective drawings, and a certain amount of hit-or-miss experimentation.

Using timbers that he cuts and strips and nails together himself, Nick is learning architecture in the most fundamental way. His house represents the ultimate leap from growing up in a space that was planned for him and partly by him, to designing and planning for himself and others.

218

Directory of Architects & Designers

Leslie Armstrong
Armstrong Childs Associates
16 East 52nd Street
New York, New York 10022

Owen Beenhouwer
P. O. Box 304
Lincoln Center, Massachusetts 01773

Kent Bloomer
Guilford, Connecticut 06437

Charles Boxenbaum
1860 Broadway
New York, New York 10023

Alan Buchsbaum
12 Greene Street
New York, New York 10013

Alan Chimacoff
Chimacoff/Peterson
134 Nassau Street
Princeton, New Jersey 08540

Michelle Gamm Clifton
Box 201
Garrison, New York 10524

George Cody
212 High Street
Palo Alto, California 94301

David Cohn
240 Waverly Place
New York, New York 10014

John K. Copelin
67 Riverside Drive
New York, New York 10024

Peter de Bretteville
8067 Willow Glen Road
Los Angeles, California 90046

Dexter Design, Inc.
133 East 58th Street
New York, New York 10022

Frank and Dagmar Dimster
927 Bluegrass Lane
Los Angeles, California 90049

Myron Goldfinger
333 East 30th Street
New York, New York 10016

Charles Gwathmey
Gwathmey and
    Siegel Architects
154 West 57th Street
New York, New York 10019

Hugh Hardy
Hardy Holzman
    Pfeiffer Associates
257 Park Avenue South
New York, New York 10010

Robert L. Harper
Moore Grover Harper
Essex, Connecticut 06426

David Hicks
7 and 8 Southampton Place
London, W.C. 1A (2A)
England

Malcolm Holzman
Hardy Holzman
    Pfeiffer Associates
257 Park Avenue South
New York, New York 10010

Lawrence Horowitz
38 West 70th Street
New York, New York 10023

Jim and Penny Hull
H.U.D.D.L.E.
3416 Wesley Street
Culver City, California 90230

Noel Jeffrey
22 East 65th Street
New York, New York 10021

Stephan Marc Klein
10 West 86th Street
New York, New York 10024

Nick Koenig
484 Redwood Road
Corralitos, California 95076

Paul Laird
135 West 79th Street
New York, New York 10024

Stephen S. Levine
1668 Third Avenue
New York, New York 10028

Carol Levy
L.S.K. Designs, Inc.
300 East 59th Street
New York, New York 10022

Ruth and Brian McKinney
McKinney Art Studio
2567 Walnut Avenue
Venice, California 90291

Charles W. Moore
Moore Grover Harper
Essex, Connecticut 06426

Judith York Newman
165 West 72nd Street
New York, New York 10023

Richard Newman
533 West End Avenue
New York, New York 10024

Richard Oliver
415 West 23rd Street
New York, New York 10011

Christopher Owen
330 East 59th Street
New York, New York 10022

Joan L. Regenbogen
176 East 77th Street
New York, New York 10021

Robert Rhodes
275 Central Park West
New York, New York 10024

Martin E. Rich
2112 Broadway
New York, New York 10023

Melissa Robbins
325 West End Avenue
New York, New York 10023

C. David Robinson
1005 Sansome
San Francisco, California 94133

James Rossant
Conklin and Rossant, Inc.
251 Park Avenue South
New York, New York 10010

Sharon Lee Ryder
304 West 75th Street
New York, New York 10023

John F. Saladino, Inc.
305 East 63rd Street
New York, New York 10021

Amy Scott
45 West 87th Street
New York, New York 10024

Barbara Simmons
10 Mitchell Place
New York, New York 10017

Henry Smith-Miller
Michael Rubin and
    Henry Smith-Miller, Architects
305 Canal Street
New York, New York 10013

Rosemary Songer
670 West End Avenue
New York, New York 10025

David Specter
2061 Broadway
New York, New York 10023

Robert A. M. Stern, Architects
200 West 72nd Street
New York, New York 10023

David Stiles
161 East 91st Street
New York, New York 10028

Alexandra Stoddard, Inc.
1125 Park Avenue
New York, New York 10028

James Swan
59 Morton Street
New York, New York 10014

Don Wall
New Jersey School
    of Architecture
323 High Street
Newark, New Jersey 07102

Carl Weinbroer
107 West 69th Street
New York, New York 10023

Whimsical Walls
Karen Sevell-Greenbaum
Iris Vanderputten
211-2 South Broadway
Tarrytown, New York 10591

John H. Woodford
Woodford/Sloan Architects
150 Green Street
San Francisco, California 94111

Joy Wulke
Fiber Works
Box 272
New Haven, Connecticut 06513

Jenny and Bill Young
Dream Beds
Box 382
Cooperstown, New York 13326

Photographers' Note

Most of the photography in this book was done with a Hasselblad. Also used were 35mm Nikons and a 4″ x 5″ Sinar view camera. Limited dimensions dictated frequent use of wide-angle lenses. The result of using a 20mm or 24mm lens on a Nikon or a 40mm lens on the Hasselblad is that it exaggerates the size of the spaces shown and alters the apparent proportions of certain objects. Minimizing these distortions is the objective of a good interior photographer. A compromise must always be made between the options of including the most possible information with an effective impression of the space and the resulting distortion.

Color film used was mostly Professional Ektachrome and Kodachrome for 35mm developed by Jack Ward. All the black-and-white photos are from Tri-X negatives developed in D-76 and printed on Kodak variable contrast paper.

About the Authors

Born in London, NORMAN McGRATH grew up in England and Ireland. A graduate of Trinity College, Dublin, he studied and practiced structural engineering before becoming a photographer of architecture and interiors.

His work is seen regularly in *The New York Times Magazine, New York Magazine, Architectural Digest, Interiors, House & Garden, House Beautiful, Vogue* and other magazines published in the United States and abroad. Some of the books in which his photographs appear are: the David Hicks series on decoration; *Young Designs in Living* by Barbara Plumb; *The New York Times Book of Interior Design and Decoration; Underground Interiors* by Norma Skurka; and *Living with Plants* by William S. Hawkey.

MOLLY McGRATH is a graduate of the University of Toronto and a former teacher and editor in educational publishing. She has written numerous articles about education, children, and parenting, and is an editor of *Baby Talk* Magazine.

The McGraths and their two children live in New York.